# Household and Economy

Welfare Economics of Endogenous Fertility

This is a volume in
ECONOMIC THEORY, ECONOMETRICS, AND
MATHEMATICAL ECONOMICS

Consulting Editor: Karl Shell

A list of recent titles in this series appears at the end of this volume.

# Household and Economy
## Welfare Economics of Endogenous Fertility

**Marc Nerlove**

*Department of Economics*
*University of Pennsylvania*
*Philadelphia, Pennsylvania*

**Assaf Razin**

*Department of Economics*
*Tel-Aviv University*
*Tel-Aviv, Israel*

**Efraim Sadka**

*Department of Economics*
*Tel-Aviv University*
*Tel-Aviv, Israel*

1987

ACADEMIC PRESS, INC.
Harcourt Brace Jovanovich, Publishers

Boston   Orlando   San Diego
New York   Austin   London   Sydney
Tokyo   Toronto

HB
901
.N47
1987

ACADEMIC PRESS, INC.
Orlando, Florida 32887

**Library of Congress Cataloging-in-Publication Data**

Nerlove, Marc, Date
  Household and economy.

  (Economic theory, econometrics, and mathematical
economics)
  Bibliography: p.
  Includes index.
  1. Fertility, Human.   2. Population policy.
3. Economic development.   I. Razin, Assaf.   II. Sadka,
Efraim.   III. Title.   IV. Series.
HB901.N47   1986        304.6'32        86-10764
ISBN 0-12-515752-5 (alk. paper)

Printed in the United States of America
87 88 89 9 8 7 6 5 4 3 2 1

For our children:

Susan and Miriam;
Ofer, Ronny, and Einat;
Ronnie, Gil, and Shelly

# Contents

# Preface

This is a book about welfare economics, but it is not a systematic treatise on the subject, although we do include a treatment of the essentials. Rather, this is a book about socially optimal population size and the social consequences of individual choice with respect to family size within each generation. Since Gary Becker's pioneering analysis, which appeared in 1960, the implications of endogenous fertility, in the sense of parental altruism towards their own children, for consumption, labor supply, and household employment decisions, have been explored extensively in the literature. The purpose of this book is to examine the general equilibrium implications of endogenous fertility for a number of issues of population policy. In our analysis we adopt the simplest possible formulation: In addition to their own consumption, the number of children and the utility of each child is assumed to enter the utility function of the parents. Subject to whatever economic opportunities and constraints they face, parents are assumed to maximize their own utility functions in making choices with respect to numbers of children and investments in them. The positive implications of this deceptively simple model are reasonably well understood; the normative implications are surprisingly far-reaching and of great importance in recent debates about population policy.

After we set out the context of our investigation (Chapter 1), we begin with a thorough review of basic principles of welfare economics and the economics of externalities (Chapters 2-3), followed by a summary of the traditional theory of household behavior and its modification to cover parental decisions with respect to fertility and investments in children (Chapters 4-5). Our normative analysis continues in Chapter 6 with a discussion of optimal population size according to various social welfare criteria. Next we turn to real and potential externalities generated by the endogeneity of fertility (Chapters 7-8). In Chapter 9, we explore the principal alternative reason for having children thought to be important in developing countries—namely, to transfer resources from the present to support the future consumption of parents in old age—and examine what difference parental altruism may make in such situations. Finally, the implications of endogenous fertility for *within* generation income distribution policies are explored. We conclude with our thoughts about the directions in which future research may be fruitful.

We hope that our book will be useful, not only to those who wish to understand the contribution which economic analysis can make to the better understanding of population policy, but also to students of welfare economics as well as economists more generally, who seek to integrate issues with respect to population size more fully into traditional welfare economics. Our book should be useful in courses on welfare economics at the undergraduate level and, more widely, among other social scientists concerned with population problems who have the equivalent technical background.

This book is the output of joint work that has been carried out by the authors in recent years. The work was performed in various academic institutions: Northwestern University, Tel-Aviv University, the University of Pennsylvania, the University of Mannheim, and the University of Florence.

This study integrates and extends scattered work by the authors that has appeared in various journals. We are indebted to the editors and publishers for permission to use material from the following:

"Household and Economy: Toward a New Theory of Population and Economic Growth," *Journal of Political Economy* (1974).

"Population Size and the Social Welfare Functions of Bentham and Mill," *Economics Letters* (1982).

"Bequest and the Size of Population when Population is Endogenous," *Journal of Political Economy* (1984).

"Income Redistribution Policies with Endogenous Fertility," *Journal of Public Economics* (1984).

"Investment in Human and Nonhuman Capital, Transfers among Siblings, and the Role of Government," *Econometrica* (1984).

"Population Size: Individual Choice and Social Optima," *Quarterly Journal of Economics* (1985).

"Some Welfare Theoretical Implications of Endogeneous Fertility," *International Economic Review* (1985).

"The 'Old Age Security' Hypothesis Reconsidered," *Journal of Development Economics* (1985).

"Endogenous Population with Public Goods and Malthusian Fixed Resources: Efficiency and Market Failure," *International Economic Review* (1986).

"Tamaño de Poblacion Socialmente Optimo," *Cuadernos de Economia* (1986).

In addition to the above, Section 2 of Chapter 7 is based on the paper by Elisha A. Pazner and Assaf Razin, "Competitive Efficiency in an Overlapping-Generation Model with Endogenous Population," which appeared in the *Journal of Public Economics* (1980).

Partial financial support from the following sources is gratefully acknowledged:

- The National Institute on Aging;
- The U.S.-Israel Binational Science Foundation;
- International Food Policy Research Institute;
- The Foerder Institute for Economic Research at Tel-Aviv University;
- Department of Economics, the University of Pennsylvania.

Nerlove's contribution was begun while he was a fellow of the Woodrow Wilson International Center for Scholars, Washington, D.C., 1980–81.

We wish to thank Eitan Berglas, Elhanan Helpman, Murray Kemp, Sherwin Rosen, Amartya Sen, T. N. Srinivasan, and Robert Willis for useful comments on earlier drafts of parts of this book. Eugenia Grohman, U.S. National Academy of Sciences, made numerous invaluable substantive and editorial suggestions. Finally, thanks are due to Stella Padeh and Madeline Dyckman for the prompt and efficient typing of this book and to Allen Schirm, Preston Ray, and Barbara Sarnecki for careful proofreading.

May 15, 1986                                          Marc Nerlove
                                                     Assaf Razin
                                                     Efraim Sadka

# CHAPTER 1

# Introduction

The ultimate difficulties of any arbitrary, artificial, moral, or rational reconstruction of society center around the problem of social continuity in a world where individuals are born naked, destitute, helpless, ignorant, and untrained, and must spend a third of their lives in acquiring the prerequisites of a free contractual existence. The distribution of control, of personal power, position, and opportunity, of the burden of labor and of uncertainty, and of the material produce of social industry cannot easily be radically altered, whatever we may think ideally ought to be done. The fundamental fact about society as a going concern is that it is made up of individuals who are born and die and give place to others; and the fundamental fact about modern civilization is that it is dependent upon the utilization of three great accumulating funds of inheritance from the past, material goods and appliances, knowledge and skill, and morale. Besides the torch of life itself, the material wealth of the world, a technological system of vast and increasing intricacy and the habituations which fit men for social life must in some manner be carried forward to new individuals born devoid of all these things as older individuals pass out. The existing order, with the institutions of the private family and private property (in self as well as goods), inheritance and bequest and parental responsibility, affords one way for securing more or less tolerable results in grappling with this problem.

Frank H. Knight (1921, pp. 374-75)

1

Malthus and the classical economists combined a very simple model of family decision making with an equally simple model of the operation of the economy. In essays published in 1798 and 1830, Malthus saw for the family procreation without bound except possibly by "... a foresight of the difficulties attending the rearing of a family ... and the actual distresses of some of the lower classes, by which they are disabled from giving the proper food and attention to their children" (reprinted in Malthus, 1970, p. 89). For the economy, Malthus said that a high level of capital accumulation induced by a high level of profits—representing the difference between output and the rent of land (natural resources) and wages—permitted a continual increase in output and population, albeit at the cost of using land of increasingly poorer quality. As a result of the model of family decisions, there was not a rising standard of living for most people but eventually a falling one. The Malthusian theory is a positive one: that is, it purports to explain, under given circumstances, what will happen. However, the classical economists drew normative implications from the Malthusian theory, namely, that unbridled population growth was a bad thing because it resulted in ever lower per capita consumption until a subsistence level was reached for most people. Simplifying, one could argue that the classical economists implicitly assumed a social welfare function (see below) in which per capita utility matters but not the number of population. We refer to this position as Millian since it was J. S. Mill who, more than anyone else, systematized and codified the classical tradition.[1] In contrast, the utilitarians, represented by Bentham (1823), held that the greatest good for the greatest number, i.e., total utility, was the appropriate goal for society.

In economic discussions, issues connected with population change have always been important in discussions of economic growth. Modern growth theorists in the tradition of Solow (1956) and Swan (1956) have developed theories of economic growth based on far more elaborate theories of the economy than the classical economists, but few theories of population growth and household decision making have gone much beyond the Malthusian model (see, e.g., Pitchford, 1974, pp. 1–10). Although natural-resource constraints may be readily incorporated in theories of population growth through the device of diminishing returns to scale in the variable factors (Swan, 1956, pp. 340–42), it is a constant proportional rate of exogenous population growth, perhaps aided and abetted by exogenous technological progress, that essentially drives the mechanism. While discussions of optimal rates of population growth or levels of population often attempt to integrate an endogenously determined population in the model (Lane, 1977; Pitchford, 1974; Sato and Davis, 1971), almost none, to our knowledge, has examined the response to changes in the economy and changes in relative prices and costs of families in deciding how many children to have and what to invest in those children's health, welfare, and education.[2] We call this household response endogenous fertility as distinguished from endogenous population.

The recognition that much investment that occurs in the economy is made in human beings rather than in physical capital and that fertility itself is shaped in important ways by economic considerations, which is crucial to the understanding of long-term growth, has led in recent years to a renewed interest in the economics of household decisions. It is at this level that decisions about consumption, savings, labor force participation, migration, investments in human capital, as well as fertility, are made. The theory of household decision making in its modern form has been called the "new home economics" (Nerlove, 1974). It has developed principally from the work of Gary Becker (1960, 1965), but most of its essentials are to be found in the earlier work of Margaret Reid (1934), and it owes a good deal to Wesley Mitchell's insights in his essay (1912) on "The Backward Art of Spending Money."

In this book we explore systematically the general equilibrium implications of endogenous fertility for many social issues of population policy, including the optimal level or rate of growth of population, real and imagined externalities, and inter- and intragenerational income distribution. Endogenous fertility means that parents care about the numbers and welfare of their children and respond to economic constraints and opportunities in their choices affecting their children. It is remarkable that this simple and obvious concept has such far reaching and significant implications. What is even more remarkable, however, is that the idea that parents care about their children does not seem to have found any place in the current ethical and philosophical debates about optimal population. We begin with a review of social welfare criteria for optimal population size and the static theory of optimal population size, optimal population growth with exogenous fertility, and the theory of endogenous fertility.

## 1.  Social Welfare Criteria

Economists usually measure individual welfare in terms of the value of a utility function that combines an individual's consumption of different commodities into a single index. Let there be $n$ individuals with utilities $u^h$, $h = 1, \ldots, n$, the arguments of which we need not specify for the moment. Individuals are assumed to make choices so as to maximize their individual utilities subject to whatever constraints or opportunities are present in their environment, including any social policies such as taxes or subsidies. A particular distribution of the arguments of the $u^h$, $h = 1, \ldots, n$, is a resource allocation. A standard desideratum of welfare economics for comparison of alternative policies affecting the allocation is the property of *Pareto efficiency*. A Pareto-efficient allocation is one in which no change, obtained presumably by policies affecting the opportunities and constraints faced by individuals, can make anyone better off without making someone else worse off. This criterion of social optimality is *individualistic* in the sense of being based on an individual's utility and is considered to be a minimal normative requirement. Nonindividualistic criteria are possible (see, for example, Tobin, 1970) but are not considered in this book.

If one considers a number of different "states of the world" resulting from alternative social policies interacting with individual maximizing behavior and attempts to rank them, the principle of Pareto efficiency provides only a partial ordering since, given a particular allocation, Pareto efficient or not, there exist many alternatives in general which cannot be compared with it according to the criterion. To achieve a complete ordering, it would be necessary to assume an analogue to individual utility functions that aggregates states of the world in the same manner as individual utility functions aggregate different collections of consumption. Aggregation based on individual utilities is called a Paretian social welfare function. Such a social welfare function is individualistic in the sense of respecting individual values, but it requires a certain comparability across individuals (see Sen, 1977).

Criteria for a social optimum usually concern choices in which the number and identity of the individuals are given; in this case, although many difficulties of comparability are involved, the criteria are otherwise unambiguous. The classical utilitarian criterion is to maximize the sum of individual utilities:

$$\sum_{h=1}^{n} u^h = W^B(u^1, \ldots, u^n).$$

We call $W^B$ a Benthamite social welfare function. Since scaling all utilities up or down by a constant multiplicative factor does not affect any essential property of $W$, if $n$ is known, this criterion does not differ from the maximization of average or per capita utility:

$$\frac{1}{n} \sum_{h=1}^{n} u^h = W^M(u^1, \ldots, u^n).$$

We call $W^M$ a Millian criterion despite Sumner's (1978, p. 107) objection that "... in its modern form the average theory was the creation of Edwin Cannan and Knut Wicksell." An alternative to utilitarianism, in either Benthamite or Millian form, has been proposed by Rawls (1971) who gives a nonrigorous argument to justify maximizing the welfare of the worst-off individual in society, the so-called maximin principle:

$$\min_{h} \{u^h, h = 1, \ldots, n\} = W^R(u^1, \ldots, u^n).$$

Harsanyi (1955) shows that if individuals maximize expected utility, the contract argument of Rawls leads to maximizing average utility if population sizes are different in different hypothetical societies, and to maximizing total utility if they are the same. An axiomatic justification of the maximin principle requires another type of argument, for example, that of extended sympathy (Arrow, 1978). If all individuals have identical preferences, maximizing the Rawlsian social welfare function leads to an egalitarian solution, but not necessarily to the highest average or highest total welfare.

When population is variable it is necessary to distinguish between social choices when all persons are potential, *ab initio*, and when the present generation exists and its size is given (Dasgupta, 1984). And, with respect to the latter, it makes a great deal of difference, as we show, whether fertility is endogenous, that is, whether members of the current generation decide on how many individuals will exist in the next generation and what resources they will have at their disposal. Most discussions of population policy deal with choices *ab initio*, perhaps because of the difficult asymmetries introduced by the fact that, from the standpoint of the present generation, future generations are all potential, but some potential people become actual in the future. This asymmetry is not eliminated by the assumption of endogenous fertility, but some of the inconsistencies and anomalous conclusions to which it leads are.

Application of the Benthamite social welfare function *ab initio* when resources are finite may lead to the so-called "repugnant conclusion" (Parfit, 1984): very low standard of living for a very large population. Suppose, for concreteness, a number of individuals, $n$, with identical utility functions that depend only on their consumption of a share of a resource, $x$, that is fixed. If the resource is divided equally among individuals,

$$W^B = nu\left(\frac{x}{n}\right).$$

Thus, if $n$ is continuously variable and $u$ is differentiable,

$$\frac{dW^B}{dn} = u\left(\frac{x}{n}\right) - u'\left(\frac{x}{n}\right)\frac{x}{n},$$

which is positive or negative according as the elasticity of the utility function with respect to consumption is less or greater than one. That is, if the utility of the representative individual does not decline rapidly enough as per capita consumption increases, $W^B$ can be increased by adding to the population. But

$$W^M = u\left(\frac{x}{n}\right)$$

so that

$$\frac{dW^M}{dn} = -\frac{x}{n^2} u'\left(\frac{x}{n}\right),$$

which is always negative, so that under a Millian criterion it always pays to reduce the population in this case. The outcome of the Rawlesian criterion depends on how one treats a person to be added to the population: if one attributes zero utility to that person if he or she doesn't exist, then he or she is the least well off person; utility will be maximized by bringing that person into existence, and the repugnant conclusion follows. But the result of maximizing the Millian social welfare function is equally absurd, leading to a one-person population (see Sumner, 1978, pp. 104–5, for additional arguments).

Dasgupta (1984) considers various ethical principles that might be used in the formulation of social welfare functions for the evaluation of social outcomes with different populations. He examines the implications of these principles with respect to three types of policy options; (1) those affecting neither the number of people nor their personal identities; (2) those affecting the identities of those alive but not their numbers; and (3) those affecting both. The plausibility of the implications of different principles differs in different contexts, and possibilities of inconsistency arise. Blackorby and Donaldson (1984) argue that a special form of a classical utilitarian social welfare function that requires a minimal level of utility for each individual resolves many of the problems associated with policy options in contexts (2) and (3).

Social welfare functions are, at least within a basically individualistic framework, a way of aggregating individual preferences. Although it would be interesting and useful to explore the implications of endogenous fertility with respect to different choices of aggregating criteria, the analysis of this book is restricted to the classical and per capita utilitarian functions and, throughout much of the book, to the more general question of Pareto optimality among members of the present generation when fertility is endogenous and when various sources of externalities prevent a competitive equilibrium from being efficient in the sense of achieving such an optimum.

## 2.  Optimal Population Growth with Exogenous Fertility

There is a large literature, artfully summarized by Lane (1977), on the comparison of alternative intertemporal sequences of total savings and population sizes. In considering problems of optimal population growth, one is concerned not merely with dividing a given pie among differently sized populations of potential individuals, but rather with the division of a variable pie among members of different generations, the size of the pie depending upon the numbers and consumption of previous generations. Population numbers over time may well be a *decision variable* in such optimization problems, jointly with the time paths of consumption. When the time path of population is given (exogenous population growth), the problem is one of maximizing some objective (social welfare) function that aggregates the utilities of individuals living at different times by adjusting the flow of consmption over time in relation to the output available. The problem of choosing an acceptable objective function is relatively straightforward, the chief issue being whether to discount the utility of future generations or not.

If, for simplicity, one assumes that every individual has the same utility function, which depends only on his own consumption, and that all income is distributed equally in every generation so that at any given time everyone's consumption is the same, and if $T$ is some finite time horizon (doomsday) after which no individuals will exist, then the continuous analogue to $W^B$ defined above is

$$W^B = \int_0^T N(t)u[c(t)] \, dt,$$

where $c(t)$ is per capita consumption and $N(t)$ is population size at time $t$. The continuous analogue to $W^M$ defined above is

$$W^M = \int_0^T \frac{N(t)u[c(t)] \, dt}{\int_0^T N(t) \, dt}.$$

The trouble with either social welfare function defined in this way is that each depends on the arbitrary date $T$, after which everything ceases to matter. As noted by Frank Ramsey (1928) in his classic paper, it is no simple matter to relax this constraint since the integrals appearing in these definitions may not converge, indeed will not converge, for all time paths of $N(t)$ and $c(t)$ of interest if $T$ approaches infinity. Although Ramsey himself pointedly eschewed it, the usual solution to the problem is to introduce a discount factor that in continuous form can be written $e^{-\rho t}$ for a positive rate of discount $\rho$. Thus $W^B$ and $W^M$ become, respectively,

$$W^B = \int_0^\infty e^{-\rho t} N(t)u[c(t)] \, dt$$

and

$$W^M = \lim_{T \to \infty} \int_0^T e^{-\rho t} \frac{N(t)}{\int_0^T N(t)\,dt} u[c(t)]\,dt.$$

The mathematical difficulty with this "solution" is that if population is growing exogenously, say at a rate $\lambda$, $\rho$ must be at least as great as $\lambda$ for $W^B$ to be defined. But as long as $u[c(t)]$ is bounded, $W^M$ will converge for any positive $\rho$. The moral difficulty with the "fix-up" has to do with the rationale of weighting future generations any less than the present one and more distant generations less than ones nearer to the present.

The question of the optimal rate of savings over time—that is, deferral of consumption by the present generation for the sake of future generations—may be considered with either criterion by introducing a production function, capital as a factor of production, and so forth. But as soon as $N(t)$, as well as savings, is taken to be a control variable, serious moral as well as mathematical difficulties arise. Koopmans (1975) writes: "A distinction should be made here between concern for the welfare of those already alive and of those as yet unborn whose numbers are still undecided. Current social ethic urges recognition of the needs and desires of living persons, within nations, and between nations—even though practice differs from norm. But there is something open-ended about the same concern for our descendents. How many descendents?" When the time path of population itself is a policy variable, arguments for per capita utility maximization generally lead to the conclusion that population should be decreased as fast as possible; the opposite conclusion is true for total utility maximization (see Lane, 1977; Pitchford, 1974; Koopmans, 1975). With respect to the latter, Koopmans writes: "... the criterion representing individuals will ... recommend a smaller per capita utility for all generations, present and future, than does the criterion representing generations. This is to be expected because the criterion representing individuals attaches value to numbers as such. ... why more people at the expense of each of them?"

We do not propose to settle these moral issues here but rather to pose questions that may add another dimension to the debate. As long as attention is restricted to static problems of population size, what Dasgupta calls the "genesis problem," the question of why the present generation is, or ought to be, concerned with future generations does not really arise. However, when the matter is considered in a dynamic setting, it becomes clear that the appropriate weighting of potential future generations, *from the standpoint of the present generation*, ought to reflect the reasons for our concern. That is, why people want children and are concerned with their welfare is a question that lies behind, and is in the same sense prior to, the issue discussed above. A satisfactory answer to this question does not resolve the matter, however. As

Dasgupta (1984) writes: "But there is no unique 'present generation.' Each future generation will in time become the present and will have to choose. So long as there *are* future generations no generation is privileged in this sense. Each generation will view the future in much the same way the present generation does its future. In particular each generation will, given the asymmetry, ... award a greater weight to its own living standard when proposing the sizes of future generations and choosing the size of the next generation. Thus in fact each actual generation will use a *different* social choice rule ... [which] will change, as potential generations become actual."

While considering the prior question of why parents want children and are concerned with their welfare does not solve the problem of an appropriate social welfare function, it does add a different dimension to the discussion, since such considerations lead one to consider *fertility*, as contrasted with population, as endogenous. When fertility itself is endogenous one can consider a *laissez-faire* path in contrast to a path imposed by a social planner in accordance with the maximization of some social welfare function, which, as we have argued, must be more or less arbitrary. The existence of a well-defined laissez-faire path permits comparison between what we call the competitive solution and the socially optimal solution with respect to the Benthamite or Millian criteria—or any other, for that matter—and consideration of the question of the Pareto optimality of the laissez-faire path.

## 3.  Endogenous Fertility: "The New Home Economics"[3]

In its most unadorned form, economics is the theory of allocation of limited resources among competing ends in order to maximize satisfaction (or utility), subject to the constraints imposed by limitations of the resources required to achieve those ends. Various elaborations and additions are necessary to accommodate this central theoretical core to the dynamics of fertility choices made sequentially over time and in the presence of uncertainty regarding future constraints and preferences. Most of these refinements, however, are necessary to the analysis of behavior, and empirical verification of the theory, at the micro level, and the limitations of the new home economics in incorporating these elements are not crucial for the uses to which we will put the theory in this book.

The first element in the new home economics is the utility function to be maximized. While its form and its arguments (what variables determine its level) are obviously crucial in determining the choices that result from its maximization, the key is whose utility function is to be maximized in connection with choices pertinent to marriage, children, consumption of commodities, work and leisure, and investment in all forms of capital.

Considering the household as already formed—a serious restriction—the utility function of the new home economics has several key characteristics. First, it does not involve the market goods or physical commodities and purchasable services usually considered in economics, but abstract goods composed of a number of "attributes" that must themselves be produced within the household (Becker, 1965; Lancaster, 1966; Muth, 1966). The importance of this characteristic of the utility function is that it leads directly to the key questions of household technology and of the composition of different types of market goods and services and physical commodities in terms of attributes contributing to satisfactions. The importance of this characteristic of the utility function is that it provides a basis for the structural content that Leontief (1947) found lacking in the standard theory of consumer behavior. That is, it provides a basis for differentiating the types of relations to be expected among different categories of goods. In particular, it provides a basis for theorizing about the household use of time and market-purchasable commodities and a basis for formulating empirically testable hypotheses concerning the relationship between the numbers and quality of children, here interpreted as a child's future welfare. Indeed, supposed differences in the time intensity of production of household goods give much of the content to recent applications of the new home economics to the problems of fertility and human capital formation. At several points in our analysis, we find that the elasticities of substitution among own consumption, numbers of children, and child welfare or quality play a crucial role in determining the expected effects of various policies. Unfortunately, applications of the new home economics have not yet resulted in the discovery of any well-founded empirical regularities that might be used for our purposes here.

A key characteristic of the utility function is that it is just that, one utility function: the welfare of the children and other members of the family are assumed to enter the utility function of a single decision maker, thus obviating the necessity of a "family utility function" with all of the concomitant difficulties of aggregation associated with it. Samuelson (1956, p. 21) has finessed this problem as follows: "... if within the family there can be assumed to take place an optimal reallocation of income so as to keep each member's dollar expenditure of equal ethical worth, then there can be derived for the whole family a set of well-behaved indifference contours relating the totals of what it consumes: the family can be said to *act as if* it maximizes such a group preference function."

Becker's recent work (1981, especially Chapter 8) has shed much light on how the conditions for a single utility function in this sense may be met. Yet the problem with the Samuelson finesse and much of its underlying justification is that it assumes a fixed family membership, and a great deal of what the new home economics attempts to explain is how that family composition gets determined. Such an explanation requires much more than Samuelson allows for in his formulation. Even Becker is not entirely consistent with respect to this issue. When, for example, are children members of the family, and thus co-determiners of the utility function, and when are they just arguments in the utility function determined for the family not including them? In this book we do not deal with this difficult issue but simply assume that, before adulthood, their numbers and welfares are arguments in their parents' family utility function. However, because children's future welfare enters their parents' utility and they, in turn, are concerned about *their* children's welfare, and so on *ad infinitum*, there is a kind of pair-wise intergenerational internalization that leads to the same type of problem at the individual level as that encountered above in our discussion of an appropriate social welfare function for intergenerational comparisons. Note that the role played by discounting in the earlier formulation is here played by a diminishing marginal rate of substitution of own consumption for child welfare.[4]

A second element in the new home economics is the technology of household production, described by a production function or functions and a list of the resources utilized in the processes involved. Typically, following Becker (1965), the inputs are time, perhaps distinguishable by household member (e.g., husband and wife) and market-purchasable commodities. The inputs are used within the household to produce the goods and services that in turn lead to satisfaction. In the simplest form in the economic theory of fertility, two time inputs (the husband's and the wife's) and one general market-purchasable commodity are assumed in the household technology to produce three household goods: child numbers, child quality, and a general commodity called "other satisfactions." Jointness in production arises not because of commodity overhead factors within the household, but because the factor inputs available to the household are subject to overall constraints. Pollack and Wachter (1975) have been sharply critical of the assumption of independent production processes, arguing both that this assumption is crucial to the derivation of most of the significant conclusions of the new home economics and that dropping the assumption leads to a failure to separate preferences and opportunities, a methodological principle that has been of great importance in economic theory generally.

The restrictiveness of the rather special assumption of separability of productive activities has not been apparent in the basically two-good (child services, defined as numbers times quality, and other satisfactions) static models usually considered. What is ruled out is complementarity among different outputs in a multiproduct context. Under conditions of variable proportions, of course, complementarity (in the sense that the output of one good could be increased without decreasing the output of the other good and without using additional resources) cannot occur if the production unit, in this case the household, is at an optimum and using resources fully. In a three-or-more-product case, however, it is possible for several of the outputs to be complementary with each other although substitutable jointly against the rest. In the latter case, holding available resources constant, increasing the level of one of the outputs optimally might well involve also increasing another, although clearly a third output level would have to be decreased. One can easily see how restrictive the elimination of complementarity could be in a context involving several dimensions of child quality, for example, health, physical development, and intellectual achievement. In a dynamic context, such potential complementaritities are of even greater significance since there is some evidence, for example, that early underinvestment in nutritional capital may substantially affect the productivity of later investment in intellectual capital.

We circumvent these difficult problems by simply introducing child welfare and child numbers as separate arguments in parents' utility functions. The cost of doing so, however, is to forgo any insight or intuition the new home economics might yield with respect to the substitution between child numbers and welfare in parents' utility functions arising from knowledge about the technology of household production, especially under different circumstances of economic development.

The third element in the new home economics is a set of assumptions about the way in which household resources, principally time, can be transformed into market-purchasable commodities to be used in the household production process. Most of what is involved concerns the terms upon which household members can enter the labor market, the wages they can earn, and, somewhat secondarily, the prices at which market commodities can be purchased. These problems are necessarily dynamic: the timing and spacing of children (with implications for their quality and future welfare), opportunities for parents' part-time work and the accumulation of lifetime labor market experience, and choices as to the amount of education to be invested early in the life cycle all depend heavily on the terms under which women can participate in the labor market and thus share in the transformation of the household's time resources into market commodities. In this book, however, our dynamics consist simply in distinguishing between childhood and adulthood, between the period during which a family has dependent children and afterwards, when they are no longer dependent.

The fourth and final element in the new home economics is the resource constraints facing a household in its production and optimization decisions. These constraints are traditionally divided into time and "other" nonwage income. While it is universally recognized that some elements of household production and consumption—sleep and food, for example—are in fact inputs into the production-of-time resources, little attention has thus far been paid to the quality of the time resources and of other family resources passed from one generation to the next. This issue is crucial to the complex issue of integenerational transfers with which we are concerned in this book. The apparently simple theoretical constraint of a time budget plus other income constraints to the household conceals beneath its serene and mathematically differentiable exterior the central problem of the continuity of society itself of which Knight (1921) wrote so eloquently.

## 4.   Where We Are Going

> "'Would you tell me, please, which way I
>     ought to go from here?'
> 'That depends a good deal on where you want
>     to get to,' said the Cat."
>
> Lewis Carroll: *Alice's Adventures in Wonderland*

Because the concepts of modern welfare economics, particularly Pareto efficiency, are central to our undertaking, we review them in the next chapter. A Pareto-efficient allocation is one in which any one participant cannot be made better off except by making some other participant worse off. We also discuss the relationship between competitive equilibrium and Pareto efficiency and derive the well-known result that, in the absence of externalities, competitive markets lead to allocations of resources that are Pareto efficient from the standpoint of the present generation. Extension of this result to the case of many generations shows, however, that Pareto-efficient solutions may be ethically unacceptable. A serious conceptual difficulty involves the treatment of those who are unborn in one allocation but would be born in another. Given an individualistic social welfare criterion, we show that every socially optimal distribution is Pareto optimal, but not every such distribution can be obtained by a competitive equilibrium. We are led, therefore, to consider so-called second-best policies, which improve social welfare but do not necessarily lead to the maximum of the social welfare function.

In Chapter 3 we discuss the conditions under which perfect competition leads to a Pareto-efficient allocation and those under which any given Pareto-efficient allocation can be sustained by a competitive equilibrium. In general, an externality arises in a situation which the activity of one agent indirectly affects the production possibilities or utilities of other agents *outside the price system*. The existence of such externalities generally leads competition to a non-Pareto-efficient allocation, that is, to what is called *market failure*. Very often, it is possible to introduce a system of taxes and subsidies that can "correct" the market. The chapter closes with a discussion of the most important source of externalities, namely, public goods, increased consumption of which may be enjoyed by one individual without decreasing the consumption of any other individual.

Chapters 4 and 5 deal with the traditional theory of household behavior and its extension to decisions about fertility. All of the basic concepts of the standard theory—indirect utility functions, Hicks-compensated demand and expenditure functions, the results of duality theory, and the envelope theorem—can be carried over to the context in which fertility is endogenous. This extension is carried out in Chapter 5, which introduces a parental utility function in which parents' consumption, child numbers, and children's welfare all enter as arguments,. The contrasting income and substitution effects on fertility, which have broad implications for our further discussion, are considered.

Chapter 6 deals with socially optimal population size when fertility is endogenous. We focus in this chapter on three social welfare functions: the sum of utilities, the average or per capita utility, and the laissez-faire case. The consequences of endogenous fertility for many issues of population policy are far-reaching. With respect to the socially optimal size of the population, we find, in both the finite- and the infinite-horizon case, that maximization of the sum of parents' and childrens' utilities leads to a higher rate of population growth than maximization of the per capita total. On the other hand, the laissez-faire solution (equivalent to maximizing a social welfare function that gives weight only to the utilities of the present generation) does not necessarily lead to a higher rate of growth than the maximization of per capita utility or to a lower rate than the maximization of total utility. The reason for the ambiguity is a direct consequence of the endogeneity of fertility for the current generation. Indeed, there is no laissez-faire solution unless children are valued directly or indirectly by their parents. We also study alternative noncoercive policies to support these various allocations, such as child allowances, interest rate subsidies, etc.

In Chapters 7 and 8 we explore the implications of endogenous fertility for market failure, i.e., the failure of the laissez-faire solution to achieve Pareto efficiency for the current generation. We find that two potential sources of externalities, diminishing returns and public goods, are fully internalized by parental fertility decisions. But parental concern for the welfare of their children gives rise to other externalities, including those associated with marriage of children and variations in the ability of offspring. We suggest noncoercive social policies to correct or offset the effects of such externalities.

When children are not valued for their own sake but only as a device for transferring resources from present to future consumption, it is well known that introduction of an alternative form of saving will reduce population growth. We show in Chapter 9, however, that when fertility is endogenous because parents care about their children, this conclusion no longer follows unambiguously because the relaxation of the constraint to saving in forms other than children creates a positive income effect.

Endogenous fertility also has implications for interagenerational income distribution policies, since such policies affect both the number and quality of individuals in successive generations. Such policies are considered in Chapter 10. For example, even if poor people tend to substitute numbers of children for investments in child quality, positive child allowances may still be optimal for redistributing income within the current generation. The optimality of child allowances as a means of income redistribution may be affected, however, by the interaction of endogenous fertility with labor-supply decisions.

We close the book with a brief discussion of the implications of our work for further directions of research.

## Notes

1.  Edgeworth (1925) alleged that Mill used a per capita utility argument to justify limits to the size of population. He argues that Mill modified classical utilitarianism in this way. Spengler (1966, p. 5) cites *Principles* (I, xiii, 2-3) to justify such a view. Sidgwick, the first edition of whose *The Methods of Ethics* Edgeworth was reviewing, certainly did formulate and reject the average theory (1874); but, as we have seen, the view that per capita utility may be a useful social criterion is clearly implicit in the Malthusian theory of economic growth and demographic change. Rawls (1971, p. 162) also attributes the maximization of the average to Mill; Blackorby and Donaldson (1984), however, concur with Sumner's attribution to Wicksell (1913). If not explicit, the social desirability of maximum per capita utility is certainly implicit in the classical position.
2.  An exception is Razin and Ben Zion (1975).
3.  This section is based on Nerlove (1974).
4.  Morishima (1970, pp. 213-25) presents an extended discussion of some of the more technical issues involved in formulating dynamic utility functions and the conditions under which such formulations can be reduced to the sum of discounted utilities of each future generation or at each future point in time, irrespective of the generation involved. In general, these conditions are highly restrictive and closely related to the conditions of Strotz (1959) and Gorman (1959) for strong separability of the utility function.

## References

Arrow, K. J. (1978), "Extended Sympathy and the Possibility of Social Choice," *Philosophia,* 7, 223-37.

Becker, G. S. (1960), "An Economic Analysis of Fertility," in Easterlin, R. A. (ed.) *Demographic and Economic Change.* Princeton: Princeton University Press.

Becker, G. S. (1965), "A Theory of the Allocation of Time," *Economic Journal,* 75, 493-517.

Becker, G. S. (1981), *A Treatise on the Family.* Cambridge: Harvard University Press.

Bentham, Jeremy (Rev. ed. 1823, reprinted 1948), *An Introduction to the Principle of Morals and Legislation*. Oxford: Blackwell.

Blackorby, C. and D. Donaldson (1984), "Social Criteria for Evaluating Population Change." *Journal of Public Economics*, **25**, 13–32.

Dasgupta, Partha (1984), "The Ethical Foundations of Population Policies." Paper prepared for Committee on Population, National Research Council, Washington, D.C.

Edgeworth, F. Y. (1925), Review of Henry Sidgwick's *The Elements of Politics in papers Relating to Political Economy*, Volume III. London: Macmillan.

Gorman, W. M. (1959), "Separability and Aggregation." *Econometrica*, **27**, 459–81.

Harasanyi, J. (1955), "Cardinal Welfare, Individualistic Ethics, and Interpersonal Comparisons of Utility," *Journal of Political Economy*, **63**, 309–21.

Knight, Frank H. (1921), *Risk, Uncertainty, and Profit*. Boston: Houghton-Mifflin.

Koopmans, Tjalling C. (1975), "Concepts of Optimality and Their Uses." Nobel Memorial Prize Lecture, Royal Swedish Academy of Sciences. Stockholm, December 11.

Lancaster, Kelvin, J. (1966), "A New Approach to Consumer Theory." *Journal of Political Economy*, **74**, 132–57.

Lane, John S. (1977), *On Optimal Population Paths*, Lecture Notes in Economics and Mathematical Systems No. 142. Berlin, Heidelberg, New York: Springer-Verlag.

Leontief, W. (1947), "Introduction to a Theory of the Internal Structure of Functional Relationships." *Econometrica*, **15**, 361–73.

Malthus, T. R. (1970), *An Essay on the Principle of Population and a Summary View of the Principle of Population*. Baltimore: Penguin. (Originally published in 1798 and 1830).

Mitchell, W. C. (1912), "The Backward Art of Spending Money," *American Economic Review*, **2**, 269–81.

Morishima, Michio (1970), *The Theory of Economic Growth*. 2nd rev. ed. Oxford: Clarendon.

Muth, Richard F. (1966), "Household Production and Economic Demand Functions." *Econometrica*, **34**, 699–708.

Nerlove, Marc (1974), "Household and Economy: Toward a New Theory of Population and Economic Growth," *Journal of Political Economy*, **82**, S200–18.

Parfit, D. (1984), *Reasons and Persons*. Oxford: Oxford University Press.

Pitchford, J. D. (1974), *Population in Economic Growth*. Amsterdam: North-Holland.

Pollack, R. A. and M. L. Wachter (1975), "The Relevance of the Household Production Function and Its Implications for the Allocation of Time." *Journal of Political Economy*, **83**, 255–77.

Ramsey, F. P. (1928), "A Mathematical Theory of Saving." *Economic Journal*, **38**, 543–559.

Rawls, J. (1971), *The Theory of Justice*. Cambridge, Massachusetts: Harvard University Press.

Razin, A. and Ben Zion, U. (1975). "An Intergenerational Model of Population Growth," *American Economic Review*, **69**, 923–33.

Reid, M. G. (1934), *Economics of Household Production*. New York: Wiley.

Samuelson, Paul A. (1956), "Social Indifference Curves." *Quarterly Journal of Economics*, **59**, 189–97.

Sato, R. and Davis, E. G. (1971). "Optimal Savings Policy When Labour Grows Endogenously." *Econometrica*, **39**, 877–97.

Sen, A. (1977), "Social Choice Theory: A Re-examination." *Econometrica*, **45**, 53–89.

Sidgwick, H. (1874), *The Methods of Ethics*, 1st ed. London: Macmillan.

Solow, R. M. (1956), "A Contribution to the Theory of Economic Growth." *Quarterly Journal of Economics*, **70**, 65–94.

Spengler, J. J. (1966), "The Economist and the Population Question." *American Economic Review*, **56**, 1–24.

Strotz, R. (1959), "The Utility Tree—Correction and Further Appraisal." *Econometrica*, **27**, 482–88.

Sumner, L. W. (1978), "Classical Utilitarianism and Population Optimum." In R. I. Sikora and Brian Barry (eds.), *Obligations to Future Generations*, Philadelphia: Temple University Press.

Swan, T. W. (1956), "Economic Growth and Capital Accumulation." *Economic Record.*

Tobin, J. (1970), "On Limiting the Domain of Inequality." *Journal of Law and Economics*, **13**, 263–277.

Wicksell, K. (1913), *Vorlesungen ueber Nationaloekonomie auf Grundlage des Marginalprinzips.* Jena: G. Fischer.

# CHAPTER 2

# Review of Welfare Economics

## 1. Feasibility and Efficiency

In this chapter, we review basic concepts in the welfare economics of resource allocation.[1] Our review lays the foundation for our discussion in Chapters 6–10 of the welfare economics of population size. We are particularly concerned with whether a given allocation of resources between children and parental consumption is efficient. Whenever gauging the desirability of a given pattern of resource allocation, the widely agreed upon desideratum is the property of Pareto efficiency. [We remind the reader that an allocation of economic resources is said to be *Pareto efficient* if it is impossible to reshuffle economic resources across the individual members of society so as to make somebody better off without making anybody else worse off.] A given social situation (allocation) is said to dominate another situation according to the Pareto criterion if in the first situation some individuals are better off without anyone being worse off. We follow virtually all economists in taking this criterion to be the minimal normative requirement for a social welfare function.

Formally, suppose there are $H$ individuals and $m$ commodities (goods and services) for consumption and production. Individual $h$ is born with an endowment, $e^h = (e^h_1, \ldots, e^h_m) \geq 0$, of commodities and consumes a nonnegative consumption bundle, $c^h = (c^h_1, c^h_2, \ldots, c^h_m) \geq 0$. An important element in a commodity bundle is leisure, which serves for both consumption and production. The excess of the endowment of leisure over its consumption is nothing else but the quantity of labor supplied by the individual. The preferences of individual $h$ over alternative consumption bundles are represented by a strictly increasing *utility function* $u^h(c^h)$ with nonnegative first-order partial derivatives:

$$u^h_1, u^h_2, \ldots, u^h_m \geq 0.$$

Suppose also that production is carried out by $J$ firms or producers. Producer $j$ uses inputs of commodities in order to produce outputs of commodities. Since an input for one producer may be an output of another, one cannot *a priori* divide the set of commodities into inputs and outputs. Instead, a sign convention is used to distinguish between inputs and outputs: a negative quantity of a certain commodity indicates that it is used as an input by the producer in question and a positive quantity indicates it is used as an output. A production plan (or net output vector) of producer $j$ is denoted by $y^j = (y^j_1, y^j_2, \ldots, y^j_m)$. For instance, if $m = 4$, then a production plan $(-3, -5, 6, 1)$ means a production of 6 units of commodity 3 and 1 unit of commodity 4 by means of 3 units and 5 units of commodities 1 and 2, respectively, which are used as inputs. The technology of firm $j$ is defined by a set containing all the technologically feasible production plans. This set is called the production possibility set of firm $j$. It is assumed that there exists a function, $F^j$, that describes the production possibility set by the inequality $F^j(y^j) \leq 0$. The frontier of this set (given by $F^j(y^j) = 0$) is called the production possibility frontier. It is assumed that $F^j_1, F^j_2, \ldots, F^j_m \geq 0$. An example of a production possibility frontier is depicted in Figure 2.1.

An *allocation* $a$ is an $H + J$ tuple of commodity bundles.

$$a = (c^1, c^2, \ldots, c^H; y^1, y^2, \ldots, y^J).$$

composed of a consumption bundle for each individual and a production plan for each producer. (Note that $a$ has $(H + J)m$ elements.) A feasible allocation is an allocation $a = (c^1, \ldots, c^H; y^1, \ldots, y^J)$ in which net outputs are technologically feasible, and together with the given endowments, they suffice for consumption:

(2.1)                          $$F^j(y^j) \leq 0, \qquad j = 1, \ldots, J$$

and

(2.2)                          $$\sum_{h=1}^{H} c^h \leq \sum_{h=1}^{H} e^h + \sum_{j=1}^{J} y^j.$$

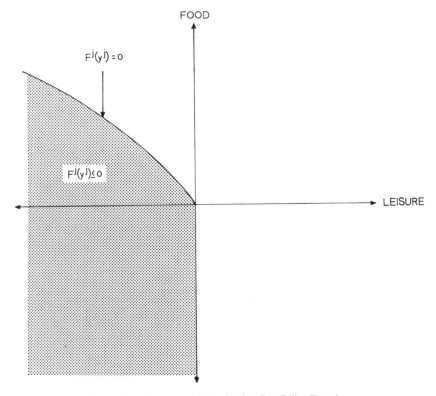

**Figure 2.1.** Example of a Production Possibility Frontier.

Observe that (2.2) contains $m$ inequalities, one for each commodity. For instance, if commodity 1 is leisure, the first inequality in (2.2) can be written as

$$- \sum_{j=1}^{J} y_1^j \le \sum_{h=1}^{H} (e_1^h - c_1^h).$$

It means that total labor input, which is the left-hand side (recall the sign convention), cannot exceed the total labor supply, which is the right-hand side. An allocation $a = (c^1, \ldots, c^H; y^1, \ldots, y^J)$ dominates another allocation $\bar{a} = (\bar{c}^1, \ldots, \bar{c}^H; \bar{y}^1, \ldots, \bar{y}^J)$ in the Pareto sense if at least one individual prefers $a$ over $\bar{a}$ and no one prefers $\bar{a}$ over $a$. To say that individual $h$ prefers $a$ to $\bar{a}$ means that $h$ prefers the consumption bundle in $a$ (denoted by $c^h$) to the consumption bundle in $\bar{a}$ (denoted by $\bar{c}^h$):

$$u^h(c^h) \ge u^h(\bar{c}^h)$$

for all $h$ with a strict inequality for at least one $h$. Then $a$ dominates $\bar{a}$ in the sense of Pareto.

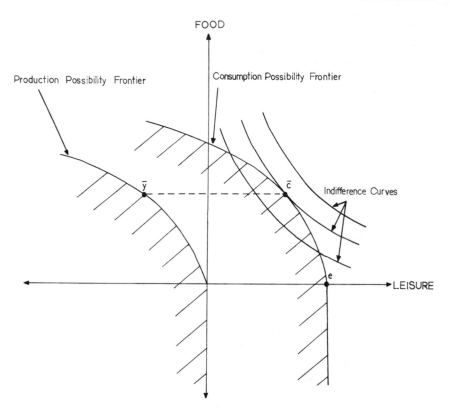

**Figure 2.2.** One-Consumer, One-Producer Economy.

Note that only the consumption part of an allocation (the $c$'s) plays a role in determining the ranking of the allocation. Firms' preferences do not exist and do not count. Consumers (individuals) are taken as the supreme sovereigns in this formulation. Also, note that not every pair of allocations are comparable according to the Pareto criterion.[2] For instance, $a$ cannot be compared to $\bar{a}$ according to the Pareto criterion if some consumers prefer $a$ to $\bar{a}$ while some others prefer $\bar{a}$ to $a$. Below, we describe more complete preference criteria that apply to all pairs of allocation.

A feasible allocation is said to be Pareto efficient if there is no other feasible allocation that dominates it in the Pareto sense. Two examples of Pareto-efficient allocations are depicted below. Consider first Figure 2.2, which describes a one-consumer, one-producer economy (the superscripts are suppressed) with two commodities. The initial endowment ($e$) consists of leisure only. If one shifts the production possibility frontier to the right by the full amount of the initial endowment, one would obtain the consumption

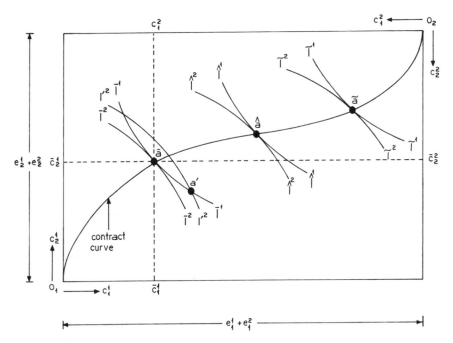

**Figure 2.3.** Edgeworth Box: A Two-consumer, One-Producer (Pure Exchange) Economy.

possibility frontier which is the frontier, of all consumption bundles that are
feasible. In the nonnegative orthant the indifference curves of the consumer
are depicted. Such a curve is a locus of equal utility bundles (given formally
by the equation $u(c) = $ constant). On the consumption possibility frontier
one chooses the consumption bundle $\bar{c}$ that lies on the highest indifference
curve. The allocation $\bar{a} = (\bar{c}; \bar{y})$ is a Pareto-efficient allocation. Observe that,
by the very construction of $\bar{a}$, the slope of the indifference curve at $\bar{c}$ is equal
to the slope of the production possibility frontier at $\bar{y}$.

The example above has only one consumer. In the next example we have
two consumers but no producers (a pure exchange economy). A well-known
diagrammatic apparatus that is often used to describe this example is the
Edgeworth box (see Figure 2.3). The dimensions of the box are the total
endowments of the two commodities, $(e_1^1 + e_1^2)$ and $(e_2^1 + e_2^2)$. Each point in
the box describes a division of the total endowments between the two
consumers, with the quantities going to consumer 1 measured from $O_1$ and
the quantities going to consumer 2 measured from $O_2$. Thus, any point in the
box is a feasible allocation. For instance, $a = (\bar{c}^1, \bar{c}^2)$ is a feasible allocation
because, by construction, $\bar{c}_1^1 + \bar{c}_1^2 = e_1^1 + e_1^2$ and $\bar{c}_2^1 + \bar{c}_2^2 = e_2^1 + e_2^2$. Curves
$I^1 I^1$ are the indifference curves of consumer 1 while curves $I^2 I^2$ are the

indifference curves of consumer 2. It is easy to see that $a'$ is not Pareto efficient because it is Pareto dominated by $\bar{a}$: consumer 1 is indifferent between points $\bar{a}$ and $a'$, while consumer 2 prefers point $\bar{a}$ to point $a'$. Since no feasible allocation (i.e., any location in the box) Pareto dominates $\bar{a}$, $\bar{a}$ is a Pareto efficient allocation. Similarly, $\hat{a}$ and $\tilde{a}$ are also Pareto-efficient allocations. The locus of all the Pareto-efficient allocations is called the contract curve. Note that $\bar{a}$, $\hat{a}$, and $\tilde{a}$ are not comparable by the Pareto criterion. Note also that although $a'$ is not Pareto efficient, it is not true to say that $\hat{a}$ or $\tilde{a}$, which are Pareto efficient, dominate $a'$.

## 2. Competitive Equilibria

Most of the welfare-theoretic literature is concerned with the kinds or methods of social organization that are compatible with achieving the objective of Pareto efficiency. In particular, the fundamental propositions of welfare economics deal with the relationships between allocations resulting from equilibrium in perfectly competitive markets and Pareto efficiency.

Before proceeding (in the next section) to establish these relationships, we describe in this section the concept of a competitive equilibrium. In a market economy, prices (of the various goods and services) govern economic activities. The various economic agents (consumers and firms) plan their actions in response to these prices, according to their preferences, endowments, and technological know-how. Prices are determined in the market-place in a way that coordinates the actions of the various agents: the supply of each commodity is equal to its demand, so that all buyers buy what they planned to, at the established prices, and all sellers sell what they planned to at those prices. Such a situation is referred to as an equilibrium. Equilibrium prices reflect the aggregate behavior of all agents. But a critical feature of the concept of competitive markets is that every participant is very, very small, like an atom, so that whatever action any one participant takes has no effect on the aggregate response, although the latter is nothing but the sum of the former. Since every agent is very small, the agent must suppose that his or her own supply or demand has no effect on the aggregate supply and demand, and therefore, that his or her action cannot influence prices; prices are parameters (signals) to which an agent reacts but cannot change.

Formally, let us denote by $p = (p_1, \ldots, p_m) \geq 0$ the vector of prices. Each individual chooses a consumption bundle so as to maximize his or her utility function, subject to a budget constraint. This constraint specifies that individual spending $(p \cdot c^h \overset{\text{def}}{=} \sum_{i=1}^{m} p_i c_i^h)$ cannot exceed individual income. The latter consists of the market value of the individual's initial endowment and the dividends paid to him or her according to his or her shares in various firms. The value of an individual's initial endowment is $p \cdot e^h \overset{\text{def}}{=} \sum_{i=1}^m p_i e_i^h$. The profit of a firm depends on the price vector (see below). Denote the profit of firm $j$ by $\pi^j(p)$, and let $\theta_{hj}$ be the share of consumer $h$ in firm $j$. Thus, the income of consumer $h$ is $p \cdot e^h + \sum_{j=1}^J \theta_{hj} \pi^j(p)$. Observe that this notion of income is not the lay notion of income, since it includes, for instance, the value of all of an individual's leisure time (say, 24 hours per day). It corresponds rather to economists' concept of full income (see Becker, 1965). In this way an individual buys leisure time (time not spent at work) from his or her total endowment of leisure.[3] The individual thus solves the following program:

$$(2.3) \qquad \max_{c^h \geq 0} u^h(c^h), \qquad \text{such that } p \cdot c^h \leq p \cdot e^h + \sum_{j=1}^J \theta_{hj} \pi^j(p).$$

Obviously, the choice of the most preferred bundle (i.e., the solution to (2.3)) depends on the price vector $p$. Thus, (2.3) gives rise to a relationship between the chosen bundle $c^h$ and the price vector $p$. This relationship is called the demand function of consumer $h$. Note that this demand is for consumption of the various commodities rather than purchases of these commodities because consumption could come also from the consumer's initial endowment, so that he or she purchases $c^h - e^h$.[4]

Consider next firm $j$. It too takes prices as parameters and chooses a production plan so as to maximize profits.[5] Recalling the sign convention, the profit generated by a certain production plan, $y^j$, is $p \cdot y^j \overset{\text{def}}{=} \sum_{i=1}^m p_i y_i^j$. Thus, firm $j$ solves the following program:

$$(2.4) \qquad \max_{y^j} p \cdot y^j, \qquad \text{such that } F^j(y^j) \leq 0.$$

Again, the choice of the profit-maximizing $y^j$ depends on $p$. This relationship is called the supply function of firm $j$. This supply contains also negative elements, which are demands for inputs. The maximum profit (i.e., the optimum value of the objective function in (2.4)) depends, of course, on $p$ and is denoted by $\pi^j(p)$. This profit is distributed in full to the shareholders according to their holdings in the firm $\theta_{hj}$ ($\sum_{h=1}^H \theta_{hj} = 1, j = 1, 2, \dots, J$).

A competitive equilibrium is a pair $(\bar{p}, \bar{a})$ of a price vector $\bar{p}$ and an allocation $\bar{a} = (\bar{c}^1, \dots, \bar{c}^H; \bar{y}^1, \dots, \bar{y}^J)$ such that

    (i)    $\bar{c}$ solves (2.3) for $p = \bar{p}$,   $h = 1, \dots, H$,

    (ii)   $\bar{y}^j$ solves (2.4) for $p = \bar{p}$,   $j = 1, \dots, J$,

    (iii)  $\sum_{h=1}^H \bar{c}^h = \sum_{h=1}^H e^h + \sum_{j=1}^J \bar{y}^i.$

Condition (i) states that $\bar{c}^h$ is what individual $h$ chooses to consume (i.e., his or her demand) at the price vector $\bar{p}$. Condition (ii) states that $\bar{y}^j$ is the production plan that firm $j$ chooses to carry out (its supply) at the price vector $\bar{p}$. Finally, condition (iii) states that the price vector $\bar{p}$ clears all markets: aggregate supply is equal to aggregate demand. (Note that $\bar{a}$ is a feasible allocation.)

## 3. The Relationship Between Pareto Efficiency and Competitive Equilibria

The relationship between efficiency and competitive equilibria that is the outcome of uncoordinated actions of millions of agents has occupied the attention of economists and philosophers for more than two centuries. In his *Wealth of Nations*, Adam smith (1776) coined the term "the invisible hand" of the market, which coordinates the actions of many consumers and producers, each pursuing his or her own self-interest, and of which the outcome is to the benefit of society as a whole.

Using the definitions above, the basic result of welfare economics is, roughly speaking, that every competitive equilibrium is Pareto efficient and that every Pareto-efficient allocation could be made the outcome of exchange in competitive markets after a redistribution of income. Leaving aside the important question of whether, or under what conditions, there exists a competitive equilibrium at all, the first optimality theorem states that a competitive equilibrium, when it exists, is Pareto efficient.[6]

We illustrate this result in the one-consumer, one-producer example discussed in the preceding section (see Figure 2.2). We now consider a competitive equilibrium in this example (see Figure 2.4). At the price vector $\bar{p}$, the production plan $\bar{y}$ is the unique profit-maximizing production plan. If one draws isoprofit lines corresponding to the price vector $\bar{p}$ (i.e., lines defined by equations of the form $\bar{p} \cdot y = $ constant), then of all the production plans on the production possibility frontier, point $\bar{y}$ lies on the highest isoprofit line. The constant corresponding to this line is the maximized profit $\pi(\bar{p})$. This profit accrues to the consumer, so that his or her budget is as shown in the diagram. On the budget line, $\bar{c}$ is the most preferred consumption bundle. Therefore, the pair $(\bar{p}, \bar{a})$ is a competitive equilibrium. Observe that $\bar{a} = (\bar{c}; \bar{y})$ is the same Pareto-efficient allocation that is shown in Figure 2.2.[7]

By its very definition, a Pareto-efficient allocation cannot be dominated by another feasible allocation, but this does not mean that there are no other feasible allocations which some may prefer to it. For instance, the allocation $a'$ of Figure 2.3, which is not Pareto efficient, is preferred by individual 2 to the Pareto efficient allocation $\hat{a}$. Thus, the fact that a competitive equilibrium is pareto-efficient does not mean that no one wants to move to some other

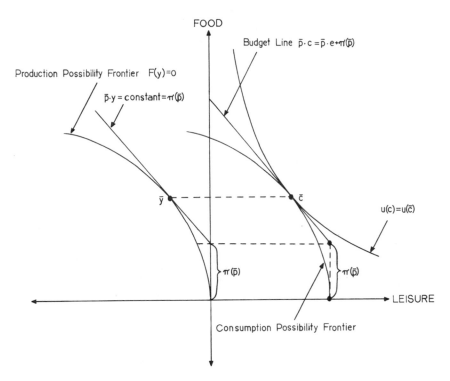

**Figure 2.4.** Competitive Equilibrium in a One-Consumer, One-Producer Economy.

allocation. In fact, even an allocation in which one person gets everything and all others get nothing is Pareto-efficient. Similarly, a competitive equilibrium may be considered by many as ethically unacceptable if a few people receive a lot and most people get very little. This consideration leads to the second optimality theorem, which states that *not every* allocation can be sustained by a competitive equilibrium. For instance, the allocation $a'$ of Figure 2.3 cannot. But observe that every non-pareto-efficient allocation (such as $a'$) is dominated by a Pareto-efficient allocation (such as $\bar{a}$). The second optimality theorem, which is confined to Pareto-efficient allocations, states that, under some convexity conditions (discussed below) every such allocation can be achieved in the marketplace through competition, after some redistributrion of initial incomes, which is determined by initial endowments and share holdings. In this sense, one can achieve any socially desired allocation which is Pareto-efficient by a competitive equilibrium.

We shall illustrate this result in the pure exchange example of the preceding section. Consider the allocation $\bar{a}$, which is Pareto efficient (see Figure 2.5).

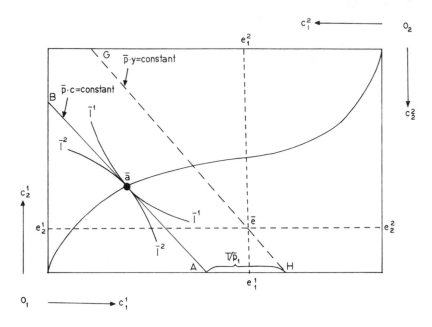

**Figure 2.5.** Pareto-Efficient Allocation in a Pure Exchange Economy.

We want to show how to get to it as a competitive equilibrium. The indifference curves of the two consumers ($\bar{I}^1\bar{I}^1$ and $\bar{I}^2\bar{I}^2$) are tangent to each other at $\bar{a}$. If one draws a common tangent to these curves (the line $AB$), the line generates a price vector $\bar{p}$. If $AB$ is the budget line of the two consumers (with origins at $O_1$ and $O_2$ for individuals 1 and 2, respectively), then $\bar{a}$ is the competitive equilibrium. But at the price vector $\bar{p}$, the budget line, which must pass through the initial endowment point $\bar{e}$, is $GH$ and not $AB$. Therefore, $\bar{a}$ is not the competitive equilibrium if the initial endowment point is $\bar{e}$. But if one redistributes income by making a lump-sum transfer, $T$, from consumer 1 to consumer 2, then the budget line will indeed be $AB$, and the Pareto-efficient allocation $\bar{a}$ will indeed be the competitive equilibrium.

Observe that a key element in the construction of $\bar{a}$ as a competitive equilibrium is being able to draw a common tangent to the indifference curves $\bar{I}^1\bar{I}^1$ and $\bar{I}^2\bar{I}^2$ at point $\bar{e}$. Being able to draw such a tangent depends on the indifference curves being convex to the origin. Mathematically, this means that the utility functions are quasiconcave.[8] Similarly, if one wants to establish the second optimality theorem in production economies (such as our one-consumer, one-producer example), one also has to assume that the production possibility set of each firm is convex.[9]

## 4.  Marginal Conditions for Pareto Efficiency and Competitive Equilibrium

In this section we characterize competitive and Pareto-efficient allocations using calculus.

Starting with the competitive allocation, consumer $h$ solves program (2.3). Setting up a Lagrangian

$$u^h(c^h) + \lambda^h[p \cdot e^h + \sum_{j=1}^{J} \theta_{hj}\pi^j(p) - p \cdot c^h],$$

one finds the following first-order conditions (assuming $c_i^h > 0$, $i = 1, \ldots, m$):

(2.5)          $$u_i^h(c^h) - \lambda^h p_i = 0, \qquad i = 1, \ldots, m.$$

Eliminating $\lambda^h$, which is the marginal utility of income of individual $h$, one obtains:

(2.6)          $$\frac{u_i^h(c^h)}{u_1^h(c^h)} = \frac{p_i}{p_1}$$

$$i = 2, \ldots, m.$$

The left-hand side of (2.6) is consumer $h$'s marginal rate of substitution ($\mathrm{MRS}_{1i}^h$) of commodity 1 for commodity $i$ (keeping utility and all other commodities constant). Formally, it is $-\partial c_1^h/\partial c_i^h$ along the indifference curve $u^h(c^h) = $ constant. Therefore, condition (2.6) states that, at the utility-maximizing bundle, the MRS between any two commodities must be equal to their price ratio.

Producer $j$ solves program (2.4). Again, setting up the Lagrangian

$$p \cdot y^j - \mu^j F^j(y^j),$$

one obtains the following first-order conditions (after eliminating $\mu^j$):

(2.7)          $$\frac{F_i^j(y^j)}{F_i^j(y^j))} = \frac{p_i}{p_1},$$

$$i = 2, \ldots, m.$$

Condition (2.7) has a similar interpretation: the left-hand side is firm $j$'s marginal rate of transformation ($\mathrm{MRT}_{1i}^j$) of commodity 1 for commodity $i$ and, at the profit-maximizing production plan, it must equal the price ratio between the two commodities.

It follows immediately from (2.6) and (2.7) that, at the competitive allocation $\bar{a} = (\bar{c}^1, \ldots, \bar{c}^H; \bar{y}^1, \ldots, \bar{y}^J)$:

$$(2.8) \quad \frac{u_i^1(\bar{c}^1)}{u_1^1(\bar{c}^1)} = \frac{u_i^2(\bar{c}^2)}{u_1^2(\bar{c}^2)} = \cdots = \frac{u_i^H(\bar{c}^H)}{u_1^H(\bar{c}^H)} = \frac{F_i^1(\bar{y}^1)}{F_1^1(\bar{y}^1)} = \frac{F_i^2(\bar{y}^2)}{F_1^2(\bar{y}^2)} = \cdots = \frac{F_i^J(\bar{y}^J)}{F_1^J(\bar{y}^J)},$$

$$i = 2, \ldots, m.$$

Thus, for any two commodities, the marginal rate of substitution is equal for all consumers, and the marginal rate of transformation is equal for all firms, and these two rates are equal to each other.

Consider next Pareto-efficient allocations. For an allocation $\bar{a}$ to be Pareto efficient, there must be no feasible allocation that entails the same utility levels as in $\bar{a}$ for $H - 1$ consumers and a higher utility level than in $\bar{a}$ for the remaining consumer. Therefore, if $\bar{a} = (\bar{c}^1, \ldots, \bar{c}^H; \bar{y}^1, \ldots, \bar{y}^J)$ is Pareto efficient, it must be a solution to the following program:

$$\max u^1(c^1) \quad \text{w.r.t.} \quad c^1, \ldots, c^H, \ldots, y^1, \ldots, y^J,$$

$$\text{s.t.} \quad u^h(c^h) \geq u^h(\bar{c}^h), \qquad h = 2, \ldots, H$$

$$F^j(y^j) \leq 0, \qquad j = 1, \ldots, J$$

$$\sum_{h=1}^{H} c^h \leq \sum_{h=1}^{H} e^h + \sum_{j=1}^{J} y^j.$$

Forming the Lagrangian of this program, it is straightforward to see that the first-order conditions are given by (2.8) above, which characterizes the competitive equilibrium. This result again shows the equivalence between Pareto efficiency and competitive equilibria.

## 5. The Social Welfare Function

We mentioned earlier that the Pareto principle is not complete: one cannot compare any two allocations according to this criterion. For instance, if Sue prefers $a$ to $a'$ while Ron prefers $a'$ to $a$, one would say that $a$ and $a'$ are Pareto-noncomparable. The formulation of the Pareto principle eschews interpersonal comparisons of utilities and thus the principle cannot rule whether the added benefit to Sue in $a'$ relative to $a$ justifies the sacrifice imposed on Ron in such a move.

However, most policy prescriptions are of the nature described above, i.e., they generate gains for some people at the cost of losses to other people. Thus, the Pareto criterion does not suffice for evaluating many kinds of policies. Therefore in most situations one cannot avoid the use of a complete social

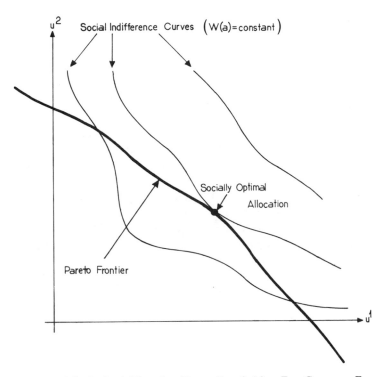

**Figure 2.6.** Socially Optimal Allocation (Pareto Frontier) in a Two-Consumer Economy.

criterion for evaluating various allocations. One is thus led to introduce a social welfare function $S(\cdot)$, to represent the preferences of society over all alternative allocations: $a$ is socially preferred to $a'$ if and only if $S(a) > S(a')$. This social welfare function reflects the ethical norms of society when making interpersonal comparisons of utilities. The social welfare function need not contradict the Pareto principle or replace it, but rather it extends the theory to those situations in which Pareto principles are not applicable. It is thus assumed that if $a$ dominates $a'$ in the sense of Pareto (i.e., at least one individual prefers $a$ to $a'$ but no one prefers $a'$ to $a$), then $a$ is socially preferred to $a'$. More generally, it is assumed that the social welfare function respects individual preferences, i.e., $S$ is an increasing function of individual utilities:

$$S(c^1, \ldots, c^H; y^1, \ldots, y^J) = W(u^1(c^1), u^2(c^2), \ldots, u^H(c^H)),$$

where $W_h \equiv \partial W/\partial u^h \geq 0$, $h = 1, \ldots, H$. Such a social welfare function is called an individualistic social welfare function.

A socially optimal allocation is a feasible allocation such that no other feasible allocation is socially preferred to it: i.e., a feasible allocation $\bar{a}$ is socially optimal if $S(\bar{a}) \geq S(a)$ for all feasible $a$. When the social welfare function is individualistic, then a socially optimal allocation must also be Pareto efficient. Thus, recalling the second optimality theorem, one concludes that a socially optimal allocation can be achieved by a competitive equilibrium after some redistribution of income via lump-sum transfers.[10]

Graphically, the socially optimal allocation is illustrated in Figure 2.6. Suppose there are only two consumers ($H = 2$); their utility levels can be plotted on the two axes. The Pareto frontier is the locus of the pairs of utility levels that the two consumers enjoy at all Pareto-efficient allocations. The Pareto frontier is essentially the frontier, in the utility space, of all feasible allocations: any pair of utility levels above or to the right of this frontier is not attainable. Observe that all the points on the pareto frontier are pareto-noncomparable. The social welfare function allows one to go one step further and ranks these and all other points in Figure 2.6, thus determining the socially optimal allocation. The social indifference curves in Figure 2.6 are curves along which social welfare is kept constant. The socially optimal allocation is the point on the Pareto frontier that lies on the highest social indifference curve.

## 6. Second-Best Redistributive Policies

We stated in the previous section that the socially optimal allocation can be achieved by a competitive equilibrium after some redistribution of income via lump-sum transfers. The redistribution can be accomplished by a direct redistribution of initial endowments or by taxes or transfers in terms of purchasing power (income). Barring slavery, it is rarely possible to transfer initial endowments. A lump-sum tax may be defined as a tax whose base is not a choice variable of any agent (i.e., the base cannot include any $c_i^h$ or $y_i^j$).

From this definition, it should be evident that lump-sum taxes and transfers rarely exist. For instance, in order to achieve the socially optimal allocation, one may need to transfer income from rich to poor people. Such transfers would be considered lump-sum transfers only if the rich do not realize that some income is taken from them just because they are rich and, similarly, the poor do not realize that some income is given to them just because they are poor. Otherwise, such a transfer is an income tax which is a tax or subsidy on the consumption of one or more of our $m$ commodities. (If the income tax applies to earned income only, it is a tax on leisure; if it also applies to interest income, it is also a tax on future consumption.)

Income or excise taxes are not lump-sum taxes. They distort the relative prices and the resulting allocation may not be Pareto efficient. To see this, suppose, for instance, that there is a specific excise tax $t_i$ on good $i$. Denote by

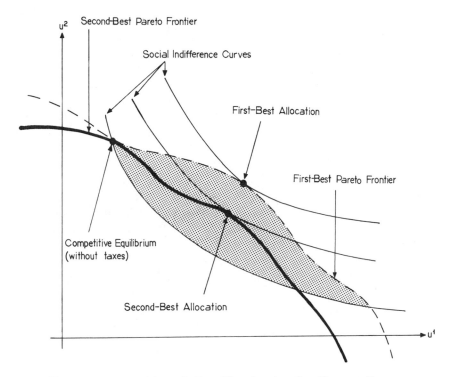

**Figure 2.7.** First—and Second—Best Allocations in a Two-Consumer Economy.

$p_i$ the producer price of this good, so that $p_i + t_i$ is the consumer price. In this case, consumers equate their $MRS_{1i}$'s to $(p_i + t_i)/p_1$, while producers equate their $MRT_{1i}$'s to $p_i/p_1$. Thus, at a competitive equilibrium, the $MRS_{1i}$'s of all consumers are equal to each other (because they all equal $(p_i + t_i)/p_1$) and, similarly, the $MRT_{1i}$'s of all producers are equal to each other (because they all equal $p_i/p_1$), but the $MRS_{1i}$'s are not equal to the $MRT_{1i}$'s (because $p_i/p_1 + t_i/p_1 \neq p_i/p_1$). Thus, a competitive equilibrium with excise taxes may not be Pareto efficient.

   Thus, nondistortionary lump-sum transfers or taxes are for all intents and purposes not available. Since such taxes cannot be levied, not every Pareto-efficient allocation can be achieved by a competitive equilibrium. In particular, it may not be possible (because of the inability to use lump-sum taxes and transfers) to attain the socially optimal allocation, which we call the first-best allocation. Still, this does not mean that society cannot do better than achieving the competitive equilibrium allocation when no lump-sum taxes are available. In Figure 2.7 we redraw the Pareto Frontier of Figure 2.6 and label it the first-best Pareto frontier. Every point on this frontier can be

obtained by a competitive equilibrium with lump-sum taxes. (The no-tax
competitive equilibrium allocation and the first-best allocation lie on the
first-best Pareto frontier.) One can see that there are many pareto-inefficient
allocations (in fact, all the allocations in the shadowed area) that are socially
preferred to (they lie on a higher indifference curve than) the no-tax
equilibrium. Some of those allocations can be achieved by competitive
equilibria with distortionary taxes or subsidies. Given a set of available (non-
lump-sum) taxes and transfers, one can find the set of all the allocations that
can be obtained with the aid of these taxes and subsidies. We call the frontier
of the set of those allocations the second-best Pareto frontier. Notice that the
no-tax equilibrium lies on this frontier. The socially best allocation on the
second-best Pareto frontier is called the second-best allocation. Thus, without lump-sum taxes and transfers, one can achieve a second-best point that,
as shown in Figure 2.7, may well be socially preferred to the no-tax
equilibrium.

## Notes

1.  As the concept of Pareto-efficiency and the possibilities of achieving it are standard notions
    of welfare economics, we refer the reader to the excellent treatises of the subject by
    Samuelson (1947), Graaf (1957), Debreu (1959), and Arrow and Hahn (1971) for more
    complete treatments.
2.  Formally, we say that a Pareto ranking is not complete.
3.  Notice that the budget constraint (2.3) can be rewritten to conform with the lay notion of
    income. Suppose that commodity 1 is leisure and that all the other commodities are
    consumer goods. Then one can write (2.3) as

$$\sum_{i=2}^{m} p_i c_i^h \le p_1(e_1^h - c_1^h) + \sum_{i=2}^{m} p_i e_i^h + \sum_{j=1}^{J} \theta_{hj} \pi^j(p).$$

Since $e_1^h - c_1^h$ is the individual supply of labor, then the right-hand side becomes the lay
notion of income.
4.  Notice that some of the elements of the vector $c^h - e^h$ could well be negative, implying sales
    by the individual; this is the case for leisure, for instance.
5.  This is what the shareholders will instruct the management to do.
6.  We explicitly assume that all utility functions are strictly increasing and quasi-concave and
    that production possibility sets are convex. We also assume implicitly that there are no
    externalities; see Chapter 3 for a discussion of externalities. The validity of the first
    optimality theorem rests on some of these assumptions.
7.  The first optimality theorem can also be illustrated for the pure exchange example of the
    preceding section, but this is left to the reader.
8.  A function $f: R^m \to R$ is said to be quasi-concave if for all $\alpha \in R$ the sets $U_\alpha = \{x/f(x) \ge \alpha\}$
    are convex.
9.  See Note 6, which is applicable here, too.
10. See Note 6; the same assumptions needed to ensure the validity of the first optimality
    theorem are needed for the second.

# References

Arrow, K. J. and F. H. Hahn (1971), *General Competitive Analysis*. San Francisco: Holden-Day.

Becker, G. S. (1965), "A Theory of Allocation of Time," *Economic Journal*, 493–517.

Debreu, G. (1959). *Theory of Value*. New York: John Wiley.

Graaf, J. de V. (1957). *Theoretical Welfare Economics*. Cambridge, Massachusetts: Cambridge University Press.

Samuelson, P. A. (1947), *Foundations of Economic Analysis*. Cambridge, Massachusetts: Harvard University Press.

Smith, Adam (1977), *An Inquiry into the Nature and Causes of the Wealth of Nations*, E. Cannan (ed.). London: Methuen 1904.

# CHAPTER 3

# Economics of Externalities

## 1. Introduction

In the preceding chapter we discussed the relationship between efficient allocations and those resulting from equilibrium in perfectly competitive markets. Under certain conditions, it is always true that perfect competition leads to Pareto efficiency and that every Pareto-efficient allocation can be sustained by a competitive equilibrium. These conditions are of two kinds. The first kind is a convexity condition, which refers to the production technologies and the individual preferences. The condition requires diminishing marginal rates of substitution in both production and consumption, and it rules out increasing returns to scale. The second kind of condition has to do with the existence and organization of markets; it requires essentially that there are competitive markets for every commodity.

With regard to the second kind of condition, suppose there are $m$ commodities, distinguished by their physical characteristics (e.g., bread, meat, clothing, etc.) and by their dates of consumption (e.g., bread today, bread tomorrow, etc.). For these $m$ commodities there are $m$ markets. But there are usually more economically distinct commodities than $m$. For example, the commodity "electricity" that is produced by a certain firm is included in the list of $m$ commodities, but it is usually produced jointly with another commodity—pollution—that is not included in the list and that has no market and therefore no price. This sort of commodity is usually produced or consumed by one agent and affects one or more of the other agents. The unpriced pollution in this example is generated by the electric company and affects (adversely) the company's neighbors. Another well-known example of an unpriced commodity, due to Meade (1952), is that of apple blossoms and honey.[1] Apple growers produce, as a by-product, another commodity—apple blossoms—which feed the bees of the honey producers. The honey producers do not pay for this benefit as there is no market for apple blossoms on the apple trees.

A common feature of these examples is that the activity of one agent indirectly affects the production possibilities or utilities of other agents outside the price system: these unpriced activities are known as externalities. When the effect is beneficial (positive), it is referred to as an external economy; when it is harmful (negative), it is referred to as an external diseconomy.

Conditions with respect to the economic environment that are essential for the validity of the optimality theorems discussed in the preceding chapter are not likely to be met in reality. The failure of competitive markets to achieve efficiency is termed "market failure." A central concern in the literature on market failure is with government policy measures that can supplement market mechanisms in a way that is conducive to efficiency. When we discuss market failures in this book, we shall confine ourselves to externalities, assuming that all convexity conditions are satisfied.

In the presence of externalities, prices no longer serve as correct signals to agents, and the invisible hand does not lead competitive agents pursuing their own self-interests to a Pareto-efficient allocation. By its very definition, an externality is unpriced. Thus, an agent whose action generates an externality does not fully perceive the social consequences of the action, since the prices the agent faces do not reflect the value (positive or negative) of the externality. Therefore, the competitive agent who acts in response to market prices does not act properly from the point of view of efficiency of resource allocation.

There are two ways of internalizing an externality and correcting this inefficiency. One way is to create a market for the externality. For example, in the Meade's apple-blossoms-bees case, one could create a market for apple blossoms in which a honey producer would pay an apple grower a competitive price for blossoms still on the trees. This price would reflect the marginal value product of apple blossoms in the production of honey. In this case, apple growers would capture the full value of apple growing, i.e., the value of apple blossoms to honey producers in addition to the value of apples to consumers, and growers' decisions on how many apples to produce (and, as a by-product, apple blossoms) would lead to an efficient allocation of resources. This way of internalizing externalities via the formation of markets is explained in detail in Arrow (1970); we do not pursue it here.

Another way of internalizing an externality is by Pigouvian corrective taxes (for external diseconomies) and subsidies (for external economies) (Pigou, 1947). Instead of creating a separate market for apple blossoms, one could subsidize the price of apples. If the subsidy is set at a level equal to the marginal value of apple blossoms in honey production (which would be the price of apple blossoms if a competitive market for apple blossoms exists), then the price of apples to the apple grower would reflect the full social value of apples and the resulting resource allocation will be efficient.

## 2. Pigouvian Corrective Pricing for Externalities in Consumption

The Pigouvian corrective pricing policy for externalities in consumption apply when the consumption of one agent affects the utility of another agent. To put it differently, in this case the utility function of an agent depends not only on his or her own consumption but also on the consumption of other agents.

For the sake of simplicity, consider the case of two consumers and two commodities. Commodity 1 is externality-free while commodity 2 generates an externality. The utility function of consumer 1 depends on his or her consumption of the two commodities $(c_1^1, c_2^1)$ and on consumer 2's consumption of commodity 2, i.e.:

$$u^1 = u^1(c_1^1, c_2^1, c_2^2)$$

and

$$u^2 = u^2(c_1^2, c_2^2, c_2^1),$$

where

$$u_3^1 \neq 0 \quad \text{and} \quad u_3^2 \neq 0.$$

Assume that each consumer views the consumption of the other as a fixed parameter beyond his or her control (parametric externality). Thus, consumer 1 chooses $(c_1^1, c_2^1)$ only, taking $c_2^2$ as given. Consumer 2 acts in a similar way. Under these assumptions, each consumer chooses the quantities to consume by equating his or her marginal rate of substitution between the two commodities to their price ratio:

(3.1)
$$\frac{u_2^h}{u_1^h} = \frac{p_2}{p_1},$$

$$h = 1, 2.$$

Also assume, for the sake of simplicity, that production is carried out by one firm with a production possibility frontier of $F(y_1, y_2) = 0$. Profit maximization yields:

(3.2)
$$\frac{F_2}{F_1} = \frac{p_2}{p_1}.$$

Let $\bar{a} = (\bar{c}_1^1, \bar{c}_2^1, \bar{c}_1^2, \bar{c}_2^2; \bar{y}_1, \bar{y}_2)$ be a competitive allocation. Then, by (3.1)–(3.2):

(3.3)
$$\frac{u_2^1(\bar{c}_1^1, \bar{c}_2^1, \bar{c}_2^2)}{u_1^1(\bar{c}_1^1, \bar{c}_2^1, \bar{c}_2^2)} = \frac{u_2^2(\bar{c}_1^2, \bar{c}_2^2, \bar{c}_1^1)}{u_1^2(\bar{c}_1^2, \bar{c}_2^2, \bar{c}_1^1)} = \frac{F_2(\bar{y}_1, \bar{y}_2)}{F_1(\bar{y}_1, \bar{y}_2)}.$$

To be Pareto efficient, an allocation $\tilde{a}$ must be a solution to the following optimization problem:

(3.4)
$$\max_{(c_1^1, c_2^1, c_1^2, c_2^2; y_1, y_2)} u^1(c_1^1, c_2^1, c_2^2)$$

$$\text{such that} \quad u^2(c_1^2, c_2^2, c_1^1) \geq u^2(\tilde{c}_1^2, \tilde{c}_2^2, \tilde{c}_1^1),$$

$$F(y_1, y_2) \leq 0,$$

$$\sum_{h=1}^{2} c_i^h \leq y_i + \sum_{h=1}^{2} e_i^h, \quad i = 1, 2.$$

It is straightforward to derive the following first-order conditions:

(3.5)
$$\frac{u_2^1(\tilde{c}_1^1, \tilde{c}_2^1, \tilde{c}_2^2)}{u_1^1(\tilde{c}_1^1, \tilde{c}_2^1, \tilde{c}_2^2)} + \frac{u_3^2(\tilde{c}_1^2, \tilde{c}_2^2, \tilde{c}_2^1)}{u_1^2(\tilde{c}_1^2, \tilde{c}_2^2, \tilde{c}_2^1)} =$$

$$\frac{u_2^2(\tilde{c}_1^2, \tilde{c}_2^2, \tilde{c}_2^1)}{u_1^2(\tilde{c}_1^2, \tilde{c}_2^2, \tilde{c}_2^1)} + \frac{u_3^1(\tilde{c}_1^1, \tilde{c}_2^1, \tilde{c}_2^2)}{u_1^1(\tilde{c}_1^1, \tilde{c}_2^1, \tilde{c}_2^2)} = \frac{F_2(\tilde{y}_1)}{F_1(\tilde{y}_2)}.$$

The interpretation of this condition is also straightforward. The private marginal rate of substitution of consumer 1 of $c_2^1$ for $c_1^1$ is $u_2^1/u_1^1$. It reflects the amount of commodity 1 that consumer 1 is willing to pay in order to secure an additional unit of commodity 2 while maintaining the same utility level. But, when consumer 1 consumes an additional unit of commodity 2, individual 2 does not obtain the same untility level (because $u_3^2 \neq 0$). Consumer 2 must give up $u_3^2/u_1^2$ units of commodity 1 in order to have the same utility. Thus, $u_2^1/u_1^1 + u_3^2/u_1^2$ can be interpreted as the social marginal rate of substitution of commodity 1 for consumer 1's consumption of commodity 2 ($c_2^1$). Similarly, $u_2^2/u_1^2 + u_3^1/u_1^1$ is interpreted as the social marginal rate of substitution of commodity 1 for $c_2^2$. For an allocation to be Pareto efficient, these two rates of substitution must be equal to each other and, in addition, their common value must be equal to the marginal rate of transformation of commodity 1 for commodity 2.

It is evident from (3.3) and (3.5) that, as long as there exists an externality (i.e., either $u_3^1 \neq 0$ or $u_3^2 \neq 0$), then a competitive allocation cannot be Pareto efficient and vice versa: a Pareto-efficient allocation cannot be sustained by a competitive equilibrium.

Let us proceed now to examine the role of Pigouvian taxes and subsidies. Suppose $\tilde{a}$ is a Pareto-efficient allocation satisfying (3.5). By the very definition of an externality, consumer 1 ignores the term $u_3^2/u_1^2$, which measures the externality imposed on consumer 2. In order to sustain the Pareto-efficient allocation $\tilde{a}$, this externality has to be internalized. Therefore, the relative price of commodity 2 that faces consumer 1 has to be corrected by imposing a unit tax $t_2^1$ (in terms of commodity 1) on his or her consumption of commodity 2. That tax is given by:

$$(3.6) \qquad t_2^1/p_1 = -u_3^2(\tilde{c}_1^2, \tilde{c}_2^2, \tilde{c}_2^1)/u_1^2(\tilde{c}_1^2, \tilde{c}_2^2, \tilde{c}_2^1).$$

Similarly, in order to internalize the externality imposed by consumer 2 on consumer 1, the tax $t_2^2 = -p_1 u_3^1(\tilde{c}_1^1, \tilde{c}_2^1, \tilde{c}_2^2)/u_1^1(\tilde{c}_1^1, \tilde{c}_2^1, \tilde{c}_2^2)$ has to be imposed on consumer 2's consumption of commodity 2.

These taxes that capture external effects and internalize them are called Pigouvian taxes. Notice that $u_3^1$ and $u_3^2$ are negative when there are external diseconomies, in which case the taxes $t_2^1$ and $t_2^2$ are positive. In the case of external economies, $u_3^1$ and $u_3^2$ are positive and hence $t_2^1$ and $t_2^2$ are negative, implying Pigouvian subsidies. Thus, the second optimality theorem can be restored with the aid of Pigouvian taxes and subsidies. Unfortunately, the first optimality theorem cannot be easily restored: not every competitive equilibrium with Pigouvian taxes or subsidies is necessarily Pareto efficient (see Starrett, 1972, for details).

Observe that the two Pigouvian taxes, $t_2^1$ and $t_2^2$, described above are not necessarily equal to each other: the excise tax on commodity 2 is individual-specific, because each consumer's unit "contribution" to the externality is not necessarily the same. There are many important cases, known as aggregate or macro-externalities, for which the externality operates via the aggregate consumption of the externality-causing good (see Samuelson, 1958).[2] In these cases, the unit "contribution" is uniform across consumers, and the

Pigouvian taxes are uniform. In other cases, a uniform Pigouvian tax is only a second-best remedy to externalities (see Diamond, 1973).

## 3. Public Goods

The commodities considered in Chapter 1 are ordinary private goods in the sense that they can be parcelled out among different consumers. Thus, if a total quantity $e_i + y_i$ of commodity $i$ is available, it is divided among consumers according to $\sum_{h=1}^{H} c_i^h = \sum_{h=1}^{H} e_i^h + \sum_{j=1}^{J} y_i^j$. There are, however, other kinds of commodities, known as public goods. As Samuelson (1954, p. 387) puts it, these are goods that "all enjoy in common in the sense that each individual's consumption of such a good leads to no subtraction from any other individual's consumption of that good." Thus, if good $m + 1$ is a public good and the total available quantity of it is $e_{m+1} + \sum_{j=1}^{J} y_{m+1}^j$, then each individual's consumption is $c_{m+1} = e_{m+1} + \sum_{j=1}^{J} y_{m+1}^j$. (Observe that $c_{m+1}$ and $e_{m+1}$ do not have an individual's superscript.) Common examples of public goods are national defense, television or radio broadcasts, basic research, weather service, airports, seaports, and roads.

Following Samuelson (1954, p. 387), we assume that there is "no mystical collective mind that enjoys collective consumption goods; instead ... each individual has ... ordinal preferences with respect to his consumption of all goods" (public as well as private). Thus, the utility function of individual $h$ is now $u^h(c_1^h, \ldots, c_m^h, c_{m+1})$. Thus, there is an element $(c_{m+1})$ that appears in all utility functions. Formally, this is also the case with externalities, and this is why we discuss public goods as a type of externality.

A pareto-efficient allocation with public goods was first characterized by Samuelson (1954, 1955). Assume again that there are only two goods, but now that good 1 is private and good 2 is public. Also, assume again that production is carried out by one firm with a production frontier of $F(y_1, y_2) = 0$. If $\bar{a} = (\bar{c}_1^1, \bar{c}_2, \ldots, \bar{c}_1^H, \bar{c}_2; \bar{y}_1, \bar{y}_2)$ is Pareto efficient, then it must be a solution to the following optimization problem:

$$\max_{(c_1^1, c_2, c_1^2, c_2)} u^1(c_1^1, c_2),$$

$$\text{s.t.} \quad u^h(c_1^h, c_2) \geq u^h(\bar{c}_1^h, \bar{c}_2), \qquad h = 2, \ldots, H,$$

$$\sum_{h=1}^{H} c_1^h \leq \sum_{h=1}^{H} e_1^h + y_1,$$

$$c_2 \leq e_2 + y_2.$$

It is straightforward to derive the following first-order condition:

$$(3.7) \qquad \sum_{h=1}^{H} \frac{u_2^h(\bar{c}_1^h, \bar{c}_2)}{u_1^h(\bar{c}_1^h, \bar{c}_2)} = \frac{F_2(\bar{y}_1, \bar{y}_2)}{F_1(\bar{y}_1, \bar{y}_2)}.$$

Condition (3.7) is known as the Samuelson rule for the allocation of public goods. Since everyone enjoys whatever is produced of good 2, the marginal benefit to society (measured in units of good 1) from producing good 2 is the sum of the individual benefits (i.e., $\text{MRS}_{12}^h \equiv u_2^h/u_1^h$). This social marginal benefit must be equal, at a Pareto-efficient allocation, to the marginal opportunity cost of producing good 2, which is $F_2/F_1$.

Public goods are usually viewed as a prime source of market failure for various reasons. For one thing, the exclusion principle may not hold: a private firm that produces a public good may not be able to extract any price for the good because it cannot exclude from the consumption of the good (e.g., national defense) those individuals who do not pay for it, "free riders." In those cases where exclusion is possible (e.g., a fenced park), individuals may have an incentive to understate their true "willingness to pay" for the public good (i.e., the true $\text{MRS}_{12}$) and thus become partial free riders.

The existence of externalities, both positive and negative, may have important implications for optimal population size. In Chapters 7 and 8 we investigate whether and in what manner such externalities could arise in the context of endogenous fertility and could, in that context, cause market failure to achieve Pareto optimality from the standpoint of the present generation.

## Notes

1.  In fact, although Meade's economics was flawless, the biological facts were wrong (see Cheung, 1973).
2.  These cases include road congestion, air and water pollution, etc. Government policies, such as tariffs, may also generate macroexternalities.

## References

Arrow, K. J., (1970), "The Organization of Economic Activity: Issues Pertinent to the Choice of Market versus Non-Market Allocation," in R. H. Haveman and J. Margolis (eds.) *Public Expenditures and Policy Analysis*. Chicago: Markham.

Diamond, P. A., (1973), "Consumption Externalities and Imperfect Competitive Pricing," *Bell Journal of Economics*, **4**, 526–538.

Cheung, S. N. S., (1973), "The Fable of the Bees: An Economic Investigation," *Journal of Law and Economics*, **16**, 11–33.

Meade, J. E., (1952), "External Economies and Diseconomies in a Competitive Situation," *Economic Journal*, **62**, 54–67.

Pigou, A. C., (1947), *A Study in Public Finance* (3rd Edition) London: Macmillan.

Samuelson, P. A., (1954), "The Pure Theory of Public Expenditure," *Review of Economic and Statistics*, **36**, 387–389.

Samuelson, P. A., (1955), "Diagrammatic Exposition of a Theory of Public Expenditure," *Review of Economics and Statistics*, **37**, 350–356.

Samuelson, P. A., (1958), "Aspects of Public Expenditure Theories," *Review of Economics and Statistics*, **40**, 332–338.

Sandmo, A., (1972), "Optimality Rules for the Provision of Collective Factors of Production," *Journal of Public Economics*, **1**, 149–157.

Starrett, D. A., (1972), "Fundamental Non-Convexities in the Theory of Externalities," *Journal of Economic Theory*, **4**, 180–199.

# CHAPTER 4

# The Traditional Theory of Household Behavior

Chapters 2 and 3 discussed the nature of a general equilibrium: as economic agents consumers and producers respond to prices, an equilibrium is defined as a set of prices such that all agents buy or sell all they wish to and markets are cleared. In this chapter we elaborate on how the responses of households are determined and on the properties of those responses.

## 1. Utility Maximization, the Marshallian Demand Function and the Indirect Utility Function

Let us consider a consumer facing a strictly positive price vector $p$ and money income $I$. In preceding chapters this income is assumed to be generated essentially as the value of initial endowments, including firms' profits. In this chapter, however, we discuss consumer behavior from a partial equilibrium point of view and take money income as well as prices as given parameters for an individual consumer.

A household attempts to maximize its utility, subject to its budget constraint. Since we focus on an individual consumer, or household, the superscript $h$ that was used in the preceding chapters to distinguish among the various consumers is deleted. Thus, a household solves the following program:

(4.1) $$\max_{c \geq 0} u(c) \quad \text{such that} \quad p \cdot c \leq I.$$

The Lagrangian of this problem is

(4.2) $$L = u(c) + \lambda(I - p \cdot c),$$

where $\lambda \geq 0$ is a Lagrange multiplier. We assume here and throughout this chapter that the constraint $c \geq 0$ is not binding and that $u_i > 0$, $i = 1, \ldots, m$. Consequently, the first-order conditions,

(4.3) $$u_i - \lambda p_i = 0, \qquad i = 1, \ldots, m,$$

are both necessary and sufficient.

Assuming that the solution to (4.1) is unique, it is denoted by $D(p, I) = (D_1(p, I), \ldots, D_m(p, I))$.[1] $D(p, I)$ is called the Marshallian demand function. The corresponding $\lambda$ is denoted by $\lambda(p, I)$.

The maximum utility attained by a consumer facing a price vector $p$ and having an income $I$ is denoted by $v(p, I)$. The function $v(\cdot)$ is called the indirect utility function and it is defined formally by:

(4.4) $$v(p, I) = u(D(p, I)).$$

## 2. Some Properties of the Indirect Utility Function

As an application of the envelope theorem (see the Appendix to this chapter), the meaning of the Lagrange multiplier $\lambda(p, I)$ can be stated in an economic sense:

(4.5) $$\frac{\partial v(p, I)}{\partial I} = \lambda(p, I).$$

Thus, $\lambda(p, I)$ is the shadow price of the budget constraint in (4.1) or the marginal utility of income.

Another application of the envelope theorem yields Roy's identity (1942):

(4.6) $$\frac{\partial v(p, I)}{\partial p_i} = -\lambda(p, I)D_i(p, I), \qquad i = 1, \ldots, m$$

or, equivalently, using (4.5):

(4.7) $$D_i(p, I) = -\frac{\partial v(p, I)}{\partial p_i} \bigg/ \frac{\partial v(p, I)}{\partial I}, \qquad i = 1, \ldots, m.$$

An heuristic explanation of (4.6) is the following: A unit change in the price of good $i$ is equivalent to a change of $-D_i(p, I)$ in income; the effect of the latter change on utility is $-D_i(p, I)$ times the marginal utility of income.

## 3. Hicks-Compensated Demand Functions and the Expenditure Function

Since $u(\cdot)$ is strictly increasing in $c$, it follows that $v(\cdot)$ is strictly increasing in $I$. Hence, it can be inverted to obtain $I$ as a function of $p$ and the utility level $u$. This function is denoted by $E(p, u)$ and is called the expenditure function. By the very definition of $E$, there is the following dual relationship:

(4.8a) $$E(p, v(p, I)) = I$$

(4.8b) $$v(p, E(p, u)) = u.$$

Since $v(p, I)$ is the maximum utility attained from an expenditure (income) level $I$ when the price vector is $p$, one can interpret $E(p, u)$ as the minimum expenditure (income) needed to attain the utility level $u$, when the price vector is $p$. Hence, one can obtain $E(p, u)$ directly by solving the following program:

(4.9) $$\min_{c \geq 0} p \cdot c \quad \text{such that} \quad u(c) \geq u.$$

(The notation here, which is standard in most textbooks, is a bit confusing: $u$ in the constraint of (4.9) serves both as a utility function on the left-hand side and as a utility level on the right-hand side.)

Given our assumptions, there is a unique solution to (4.9). Denote this solution by $H(p, u) = (H_1(p, u), \ldots, H_m(p, u))$. It is called the Hicks-compensated demand function, because, for a given $u$, $H(\cdot)$ describes the change in $c$ resulting from a change in $p$ that is accompanied by a Hicks compensation in income (expenditure), which is needed in order to keep utility constant. One can then define $E(p, u)$ directly by

(4.10) $$E(p, u) = p \cdot H(p, u).$$

## 4. Some Properties of the Expenditure Function

Again by applying the envelope theorem, one can obtain the derivative property of the expenditure function:

(4.11) $$\frac{\partial E(p, u)}{\partial p_i} = H_i(p, u), \quad i = 1, \ldots, m,$$

i.e., the change in the minimum expenditure necessitated by a unit change in the price of good $i$ is equal to the Hicks-compensated demand for that good.

Using the definition of $E(p, u)$ as the minimum expenditure needed to attain a utility level $u$ at a price vector, $p$, one can show that $E(p, u)$ is concave in $p$. To prove this, let $\bar{p}$ and $\tilde{p}$ be two price vectors and let $0 < \alpha < 1$. Then

$$E(\alpha\bar{p} + (1 - \alpha)\tilde{p}, u) = (\alpha\bar{p} + (1 - \alpha)\tilde{p}) \cdot H(\alpha\bar{p} + (1 - \alpha)\tilde{p}, u)$$

$$= \alpha\bar{p} \cdot H(\alpha\bar{p} + (1 - \alpha)\tilde{p}, u)$$
$$+ (1 - \alpha)\tilde{p} \cdot H(\alpha\bar{p} + (1 - \alpha)\tilde{p}, u)$$

$$\geq \alpha\bar{p} \cdot H(\bar{p}, u) + (1 - \alpha)\tilde{p} \cdot H(\tilde{p}, u)$$

$$= \alpha E(\bar{p}, u) + (1 - \alpha)E(\tilde{p}, u),$$

where the inequality sign follows from the definitions of $H(\bar{p}, u)$ and $H(\tilde{p}, u)$ as the expenditure-minimizing-bundles at the price vectors $\bar{p}$ and $\tilde{p}$, respectively.

Since $E(p, u)$ is concave in $p$, it follows that the matrix $(\partial^2 E/\partial p_i \partial p_j)$ of its second-order derivatives with respect to prices is symmetric and negative semidefinite.[2] Using the derivative property of $E$ (4.11), the matrix $(\partial H_i/\partial p_j)$, which is called the Hicks-Slutsky substitution matrix, is symmetric and negative semidefinite. In particular, it follows that the own-substitution effects, $\partial H_i/\partial p_i$, are nonpositive and that the cross-substitution effects are symmetric: $\partial H_i/\partial p_j = \partial H_j/\partial p_i$.

## 5. The Relationship between the Hicks-Compensated and the Marshallian Demand Functions

Consider a price vector $p$ and an income level $I$. These describe a budget line shown in Figure 4.1. On this budget line, a utility-maximizing consumer chooses the bundle $D(p, I)$ and attains the utility level $v(p, I)$. Recall that $H(p, v(p, I))$ is the expenditure-minimizing bundle required to attain the level of utility $v(P, I)$ at the price vector $p$. As the figure shows,

$$(4.12) \qquad D_i(P, I) = H_i(p, v(p, I)), \qquad i = 1, \ldots, m.$$

In a similar way, one can show that

$$(4.13) \qquad H_i(p, u) = D_i(p, E(p, u)), \qquad i = 1, \ldots, m.$$

A very useful decomposition of the price effect on the Marshallian demand is described by the Hicks-Slutsky equations:

$$(4.14) \qquad \frac{\partial D_i(p, I)}{\partial p_j} = \frac{\partial H_i(p, v(p, I))}{\partial p_j} - D_j(p, I)\frac{\partial D_i(p, I)}{\partial I}, \qquad i, j = 1, \ldots, m.$$

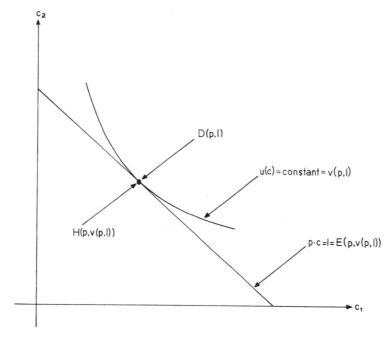

**Figure 4.1.** Consumer Choice in a Two-Good World.

These equations state that the price effect on the Marshallian demand $(\partial D_i/\partial p_j)$ can be decomposed into two effects: a Hicks-Slutsky substitution effect, $\partial H_i/\partial p_j$, and an income affect, $(-)D_j\partial D_i/\partial I$. The first effect describes what happens to the quantity demanded of good $i$ when income is adjusted so as to keep the utility level constant. The second effect states that a unit change in the price of good $j$ is equivalent to a change of $-D_j$ in real income, which induces a change of $-D_j\partial D_i/\partial I$ in the quantity demanded of good $i$ (see Hicks, 1936; Slutsky, 1915).

To prove (4.14), differentiate (4.13) with respect to $p_j$:

$$\frac{\partial H_i(p, u)}{\partial p_j} = \frac{\partial D_i(p, E(p, u))}{\partial p_j} + \frac{\partial D_i(p, E(p, u))}{\partial I} \frac{\partial E(p, u)}{\partial p_j}.$$

Using the derivative property of the expenditure function (4.11), one obtains:

$$(4.15) \qquad \frac{\partial D_i(p, E(p, u))}{\partial p_j} = \frac{\partial H_i(p, u)}{\partial p_j} - \frac{H_i(p, u)\partial D_i(p, E(p, u))}{\partial I}.$$

The equation (4.15) is true for all $u$. In particular, it holds for $u = v(p, I)$ or $I = E(p, u)$. Substituting the latter relationships and (4.12) into (4.15) yields the Hicks-Slutsky equations (4.14).

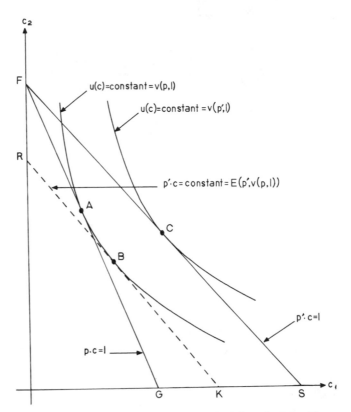

**Figure 4.2.** Hicks–Slutsky Decomposition of the Effect of a Price Change.

The Hicks-Slutsky decomposition is described graphically in Figure 4.2. Start from a price vector $p$ and a budget line FAG and then reduce the price of good 1 and move to a price vector $p'$ and a budget line FCS. The full price effects, $\partial D_1/\partial p_1$ and $\partial D_2/\partial p_1$, are described by the move from A to C. Making a Hicks compensation (negative in this case because the price of good 1 was lowered rather than raised) yields the budget line RBK, given by the equation $p' \cdot c = E(p', V(p, I))$. The substitution effects, $\partial H_1/\partial p_1$ and $\partial H_2/\partial p_2$, are thus described by the move from A to B. The change in real income induced by the fall in prices from $p$ to $p'$ is described by a shift from the budget line RBK to the budget line FCS. The income effects, $-D_1\partial D_1/\partial I$ and $-D_1\partial D_2/\partial I$, are described by the move from B to C.

The indirect utility function and the notion of income-compensated demand functions play a key role in the elaboration of the basic theory of consumer behavior and its extension to fertility decision, to which we turn in the next chapter.

**Appendix: The Envelope Theorem**

Consider the following constrained optimization problem

$$\max_{x_1, \ldots, x_m} F(x_1, \ldots, x_m; \alpha_1, \ldots, \alpha_r)$$

$$\text{s.t.:}$$
$$G(x_1, \ldots, x_m; \alpha_1, \ldots, \alpha_r) = 0,$$

where $\alpha = (\alpha_1, \ldots, \alpha_r)$ is a vector of parameters. Suppose that there exists a unique solution to this problem and denote it by $x(\alpha) = (x_1(\alpha), \ldots, x_m(\alpha))$. Also, denote the corresponding Lagrangian multiplier by $\lambda(\alpha)$. Define by $v(\alpha)$ the maximum attainable value of $F$, i.e.,

$$v(\alpha) = F(x(\alpha); \alpha).$$

*The Envelope Theorem*:

$$\frac{\partial v(\alpha)}{\partial \alpha_i} = \frac{\partial F(x(\alpha); \alpha)}{\partial \alpha_i} + \lambda(\alpha) \frac{\partial G(x(\alpha); \alpha)}{\partial \alpha_i}, \qquad i = 1, \ldots, r.$$

The proof follows by a straightforward application of the first-order conditions and can be found in many textbooks (e.g., Varian, 1978).

**Notes**

1.  A sufficient condition for uniqueness is strict quasi-concavity of $u$ (i.e., the indifference surfaces are strictly convex to the origin). Formally, if $u(\bar{c}) \geq u(\tilde{c})$, then $u(\alpha\bar{c} + (1 - \alpha)\tilde{c}) > u(\tilde{c})$ for all $\bar{c}, \tilde{c}$ and $0 < \alpha < 1$.
2.  An $m \times m$ matrix, $B = (b_{ij})$, is symmetric if $b_{ij} = b_{ji}$ for all $i, j = 1, \ldots, m$. A symmetric matrix, $B = (b_{ij})$, is negative semidefinite if $\sum_{i=1}^{m} \sum_{j=1}^{m} b_{ij} x_i x_j \leq 0$ for all vectors $x = (x_1, \ldots, x_m)$.

**References**

Hicks, J. R. (1936), *Value and Capital*. Oxford: Clarendon.
Roy, R. (1942), *De l'Utilité, Contribution à la Théorie des Choix*. Paris: Herman.
Slutsky, E. (1915), "Sulla Teoria del Bilancio del Consomatore," *Giornale degli Economisti*: **51**, 1–26. English translation in G. J. Stigler and K. E. Boulding (eds.), *Readings in Price Theory*. Homewood, Illinois: Richard D. Irwin, 1952.
Varian, H. (1978), *Microeconomic Analysis*. New York: W. W. Norton.

# CHAPTER 5

# Household Behavior with Endogenous Fertility

A distinguishing feature of the approach adopted in this book is that parents care about the welfare and numbers of their children. Also, these two variables are controlled, at least partly, by the parents. This feature introduces nonlinearities and nonconvexities into the budget constraint and destroys some conventional characteristics of the utility function. This chapter analyzes consumer behavior under these circumstances.

## 1. A Generalized Model of Consumer Choice

Consider a pair of parents as an individual decision maker who consumes units of a single composite consumption good ($c$). The parents also extract utility from the number of their children ($n$) and the quality, or well-being ($z$), of each one of them. This quality is measured by the units of the single composite good spent on these children (e.g., on their education, health, etc.). For the sake of simplicity, we treat $n$ as a continuous variable. In addition, we assume that all children are identical and that the parents treat them symmetrically, so we use the symbol $z$ for the quality of every child.

The parents have an ordinary utility function,

(5.1) $$\tilde{u}(c, z, n),$$

where $\tilde{u}_i > 0$, $i = 1, 2, 3$. This means that the parents extract positive utility from all three variables—$c$, $z$, and $n$. The parents choose both $z$ and $n$ in addition to $c$. Let the parents' income, in terms of the single composite good, be $I$. They spend $c$ on themselves and a total of $zn$ on their children. We also allow for a pecuniary benefit from each child, denoted by $\beta$ and measured in terms of the single composite good. This benefit could be a child allowance paid by the government, a wage earned by the child and contributed to the household income, etc. The benefit could also be negative if there is a tax on children. Thus, the parents' budget constraint is:

(5.2) $$c + zn \leq I + \beta n.$$

The term $zn$ makes the budget constraint nonlinear. Furthermore, the budget set $\{(c, z, n) \mid c + zn \leq I + \beta n\}$, describing the parents' feasible bundles of $c$, $z$, and $n$, is not convex. Notice, however, that the utility function (5.1) can still have all the conventional properties, such as increasing monotonicity and quasi-concavity.

The analysis and results of the preceding chapter hold for a linear budget constraint but can be applied to this case with some transformation.[1] We assume throughout that the utility function is monotonically increasing and strictly quasi-concave, but these assumptions on the utility function are not necessary. In fact, as long as the Marshallian and Hicksian demand functions are well defined and differentiable, the results of Chapter 4 hold. For this reason, it is useful to redefine the choice variables of the consumer unit so as to obtain a linear budget constraint at the expense of losing the conventional properties of the utility function. Once this is done, the results of Chapter 4 apply with respect to the newly defined variables.

Specifically, defining by $q$ the total expenditure on children (i.e., $q = zn$) and letting

(5.3) $$u(c, q, n) = \tilde{u}(c, q/n, n),$$

the parents' optimization problem is to choose $c$, $q$, and $n$ so as to maximize (5.3) subject to the following linear budget constraint:

(5.4) $$c + q \leq I + \beta n.$$

Observe that while $\tilde{u}$ is monotonically increasing in its third argument, $n$ (i.e., $\tilde{u}_3 > 0$), it follows from (5.3) that $u$ need not increase in $n$ because of the term $q/n$ in $\tilde{u}$:

$$u_3 = \tilde{u}_3 - q\tilde{u}_2/n^2.$$

Furthermore, the number of children in the budget constraints (5.4) appears in the same way as the labor supply appears in a conventional model, i.e., it adds to income rather than to expenditures (assuming $\beta > 0$). Thus, at the parents' optimum, the marginal utility of $n$ (namely, $u_3$) must be negative. With this linear budget constraint, all the results of the preceding chapter hold with respect to the variables $c$, $q$, and $n$.

## 2. The Effect of Income on Fertility

An interesting question in this context of endogenous fertility is whether a rich family will have more children than a poor family. This issue was investigated by Becker and Lewis (1973). Notice that this question is not as simple as in a standard consumer demand analysis in which one asks whether a certain commodity is normal or inferior. To see this, consider first the consumer optimization problem in terms of the original utility function, $\tilde{u}$, and the nonlinear budget constraint (5.2):

$$(5.5) \qquad \max_{c, z, n} \tilde{u}(c, z, n), \qquad \text{such that} \qquad c + zn \leq I.$$

(To simplify the analysis and make it comparable to that of Becker and Lewis, we let $\beta = 0$.) One can see that the quality of children ($z$) is the "price" of the quantity of children ($n$) and vice versa. Thus, some of the parents' choice variables also act as prices, and the usual conditions on the utility function that guarantee the normality of a certain good (e.g., Samuelson, 1947) do not apply. New conditions must be derived.

The optimal $c$, $z$, and $n$ in the problem (5.5) all depend on income $I$. Denote the optimal $c$, $z$, and $n$ by $C(I)$, $Z(I)$, and $N(I)$, respectively; one is interested in the sign of the elasticity of $N$ with respect to $I$. As we noted, this is not the standard question as to whether a certain good is a normal good, and one cannot use the standard conditions for normality. Therefore, we form a hypothetical problem that is a standard consumer optimization problem; we explain below how it is related to our true problem, (5.5).

Consider the following problem:

$$(5.6) \qquad \max_{c, z, n} \tilde{u}(c, z, n), \qquad \text{such that} \qquad c + p_z z + p_n n \leq I + M,$$

where $p_z > 0$, $p_n > 0$, and $M$ are parameters.[2] One can interpret $p_z$ and $p_n$ as the "prices" of quality and quantity of children, respectively; $M$ is interpeted as a lump-sum transfer. Now (5.6) is a standard consumer optimization problem, and one denotes the optimal bundle of $c$, $z$, and $n$ by $\bar{C}(p_z, p_n, I + M)$, $\bar{Z}(p_z, p_n, I + M)$, and $\bar{N}(p_z, p_n, I + M)$, respectively. The latter functions are conventional Marshallian demand functions and, in particular, it is assumed that they exhibit normality:

$$\bar{C}_3, \bar{Z}_3, \bar{N}_3 > 0.$$

Comparing (5.5) with (5.6), it is straightforward to establish the relationship between $(C, Z, N)$ and $(\bar{C}, \bar{Z}, \bar{N})$. Evaluated at $p_z = N(I)$, $p_n = Z(I)$ and $M = N(I)Z(I)$, the bundle $(\bar{C}, \bar{Z}, \bar{N})$ is equal to $(C, Z, N)$:

(5.7a)                      $\bar{C}(N(I), Z(I), I + N(I)Z(I)) = C(I),$

(5.7b)                      $\bar{Z}(N(I), Z(I), I + N(I)Z(I)) = Z(I),$

(5.7c)                      $\bar{N}(N(I), Z(I), I + N(I)Z(I)) = N(I).$

Differentiating totally the last two relationships with respect to $I$:

(5.8a)            $(\bar{Z}_1 + Z\bar{Z}_3)\dfrac{dN}{dI} + (\bar{Z}_2 + N\bar{Z}_3 - 1)\dfrac{dZ}{dI} = -\bar{Z}_3.$

(5.8b)            $(\bar{N}_1 + Z\bar{N}_3 - 1)\dfrac{dN}{dI} + (\bar{N}_2 + N\bar{N}_3)\dfrac{dZ}{dI} = -\bar{N}_3.$

Employing the Hicks-Slutsky equations corresponding to the hypothetical problem (5.6), one sees that $\bar{Z}_1 + Z\bar{Z}_3$ is the Hicks-Slutsky substitution effect of the "price" of the quality of children on the quantity of children demanded. Denote this effect by $\bar{S}_{zz}$. Also, $\bar{Z}_2 + N\bar{Z}_3$ is the Hicks-Slutsky substitution effect of the "price" of the quantity of children on the quality of children demanded; denote it by $\bar{S}_{zn}$. Similarly, $\bar{N}_1 + Z\bar{N}_3 = \bar{S}_{nz}$, and $\bar{N}_2 + N\bar{N}_3 = \bar{S}_{nn}$. By the symmetry of the Hicks-Slutsky effects, $\bar{S}_{zn} = \bar{S}_{nz}$. Substituting these relationships into (5.8) and solving for $dN/dI$:

(5.9)                      $\dfrac{dN}{dI} = \dfrac{\bar{N}_3(1 - \bar{S}_{nz}) + \bar{Z}_3\bar{S}_{nn}}{(1 - \bar{S}_{nz})^2 - \bar{S}_{zz}\bar{S}_{nn}}.$

In elasticity terms, (5.9) becomes

(5.10)                      $\eta_{nI} = k\dfrac{\bar{\eta}_{nI}(1 - \bar{\varepsilon}_{nz}) + \bar{\eta}_{zI}\bar{\varepsilon}_{nn}}{(1 - \bar{\varepsilon}_{nz})^2 - \bar{\varepsilon}_{zz}\bar{\varepsilon}_{nn}},$

where:

$\eta_{nI} = \dfrac{dN}{dI}\cdot\dfrac{I}{N}$, income elasticity of $N(I)$,

$\bar{\eta}_{nI} = \bar{N}_3\dfrac{I + N\bar{Z}}{\bar{N}}$, income elasticity of $\bar{N}(\cdot, \cdot, \cdot)$ (assumed positive)

$\bar{\eta}_{zI} = \bar{Z}_3\dfrac{I + N\bar{Z}}{\bar{Z}}$, income elasticity of $\bar{Z}(\cdot, \cdot, \cdot)$ (assumed positive)

$$k = \frac{I}{I + \bar{N}\bar{Z}} < 1,$$

$$\bar{\varepsilon}_{nn} \equiv \frac{\bar{S}_{nn}p_n}{\bar{N}} = \frac{\bar{S}_{nn}\bar{Z}}{\bar{N}}, \text{ own-substitution elasticity of } \bar{N}(\cdot, \cdot, \cdot),$$

$$\bar{\varepsilon}_{zz} \equiv \frac{\bar{S}_{zz}p_z}{\bar{Z}} = \frac{\bar{S}_{zz}\bar{N}}{\bar{Z}}, \text{ own-substitution elasticity of } \bar{Z}(\cdot, \cdot, \cdot),$$

$$\bar{\varepsilon}_{nz} \equiv \frac{\bar{S}_{nz}p_z}{\bar{N}} = \bar{S}_{nz}, \text{ cross-substitution elasticity.}$$

Similarly, we find that

(5.11) $$\eta_{zI} = k \frac{\bar{\eta}_{zI}(1 - \bar{\varepsilon}_{nz}) + \bar{n}_{nI}\bar{\varepsilon}_{zz}}{(1 - \bar{\varepsilon}_{nz})^2 - \bar{\varepsilon}_{zz}\bar{\varepsilon}_{nn}}.$$

Thus, one can see from (5.10) that if there is a unitary substitution elasticity between the quantity and quality of children (i.e., $\bar{\varepsilon}_{nz} = 1$), then $\eta_{nI} = -(k/\bar{\varepsilon}_{zz})\bar{\eta}_{zI} > 0$, by the negativity of own-substitution elasticity, $\bar{\varepsilon}_{zz}$, and the normality of $\bar{Z}$ ($\bar{\eta}_{zI} > 0$). In this case an increase in income increases fertility (and, as can be seen from (5.11), child quality as well).

Now assume that the substitution elasticity between the quantity and quality of children is larger than 1 (i.e., $\bar{\varepsilon}_{nz} > 1$). Also assume that total expenditure on children increases with income (i.e., $N(I)Z(I)$ increases in $I$). This means that at least one of the components of this expenditure, $N(I)$ or $Z(I)$, must be increasing in income. Suppose then that $\eta_{zI} > 0$. Since it is assumed that $\bar{\varepsilon}_{nz} > 1$, it follows that the numerator on the right-hand side of (5.11) is negative. Hence the denominator must also be negative. But it then follows from (5.10) that $\eta_{nI}$ is positive. Thus, under the assumption that total expenditure on children increases in income, a high degree of substitutability between child quality and quantity (i.e., $\bar{\varepsilon}_{nz} > 1$) implies that income has a positive effect on both the quantity and the quality of children (i.e., both $\eta_{nI}$ and $\eta_{zI}$ are positive).

However, as this quantity-quality problem is not a standard consumer choice problem, one can extract from (5.10) many cases in which income has a negative effect on fertility (i.e., $\eta_{nI} < 0$). If the substitution elasticity between the quantity and quality of children is smaller than one ($\bar{\varepsilon}_{nz} < 1$), there are two possibilities.

One possibility is that the denominator of (5.10) or (5.11) is positive. This occurs when the own-substitution elasticities ($\bar{\varepsilon}_{zz}$ and $\bar{\varepsilon}_{nn}$) are relatively low. In this case one can see from (5.10) that if the income elasticity of quality in the hypothetical problem (5.6) (namely, $\bar{\eta}_{zI}$) is substantially higher than the income elasticity of quantity in the same problem (namely, $\bar{\eta}_{nI}$), then child quantity falls with income ($\eta_{nI} < 0$) while child quality rises ($\eta_{ZI} > 0$).[3]

The other possibility is that the denominator of (5.10) or (5.11) is negative. This occurs when the own-substitution elasticities ($\bar{\varepsilon}_{zz}$ and $\bar{\varepsilon}_{nn}$) are relatively high. In this case, if $\bar{\eta}_{zI}$ is substantially lower than $\bar{\eta}_{nI}$, then, again, $\eta_{nI} < 0$ and $\eta_{zI} > 0$.

## 3. Conclusion

Introducing the quantity and "quality" of children in parents' utility function introduces a nonlinearity and nonconvexity in the budget constraint. However, a reformulation in which the budget constraint is linear but the utility function is no longer monotonically increasing and strictly quasi-concave permits us to apply the conventional theory of consumer choice to derive the results of Becker and Lewis (1973). The principal result is that, even if the income elasticities of demand for both quantity and quality of children are positive, the observed (uncompensated) elasticity of fertility (numbers of children) with respect to income may be negative. Whether or not this occurs depends in part on the elasticity of substitution between quantity and quality of children in parents utility function. This result is important to our analysis of the laissez-faire choices of parents in Chapters 7–10.

## Notes

1. Some extensions of these results for nonlinear budget constraints can be found in Epstein (1981).
2. This formulation is due to Becker and Lewis (1973). However, the analysis that follows here differs from theirs, and we derive different conditions.
3. This possibility concerning differences between the income elasticities of child quality and quantity was noted by Becker and Lewis (1973).

## References

Becker, G. S. and H. G. Lewis (1973). "On the Interaction Between the Quantity and Quality of Children," *Journal of Political Economy*, **81**, 279–288.

Epstein, L. G. (1981). "Generalized Duality and Integrability," *Econometrica*, **49**, 655–78.

Samuelson, P. A. (1947), *Foundations of Economic Analysis*. Cambridge, Massachusetts: Harvard University Press.

# CHAPTER 6

# Socially Optimal Population Size

In this chapter we examine the implications for optimal population sizes of several social welfare criteria and the policies that are needed to achieve those optima.

## 1. Criteria for Social Optima with Variable Population

The traditional social welfare function discussed in Chapter 2 takes for granted the existence of individuals. In fact, as Sumner (1978, p. 95) notes, "most of the traditional moral theories ... were devised in and for a world in which population was not a pressing problem." This social welfare function is concerned with the allocation of resources among the existing population. It deals with what is referred to as fixed pool problems. However, in this book, the number of persons are to be determined as part of the analysis. This kind of problem can be referred to as a variable pool problem.

It is not clear that a social welfare function, which works very nicely for a fixed pool problem, would also work reasonably well for variable pool problems. Sumner (1978, p. 96) claims that "many classical theories are incomplete in just this sense: they imply little or nothing for population problems. Utilitarianism is an exception to this rule: it may generate what one regards as the wrong solution, but it at least generates a solution."

The utilitarian theory has two versions. The original one (classical utilitarianism) was first enumerated in modern form by Bentham and given further refinement by Sidgewick. Bentham and Sidgewick argued that if additional people enjoy, on the whole, positive happiness (utility), population ought to be allowed to increase to the point at which total utility (the sum of the utilities of all people) is at a maximum. A revised version of the classical theory is known as average utilitarianism. It is concerned not with total utility, but rather with a maximization of the average, or per capita, utility. Edgeworth (1925) attributes this version to Mill, who used a per capita utility maximization argument to justify limits to the size of population.[1] In the remainder of this section we give a brief summary of the literature concerned with the debate between the advocates of the two theories—classical utilitarianism and average utilitarianism.

To begin with, note the obvious fact that there is no difference between the two theories in situations concerning the choice among alternatives that have the same effects on population levels: if population is constant, the average utility differs from the total utility by a multiplicative constant. Thus, it is only in a situation in which different alternatives would produce different population levels that the two theories can diverge. Consider the following example from Sumner (1978, p. 100): Suppose that the question is whether to add an additional person to the existing population. If the utility added by the additional person is positive but less than the *status quo* average, "... then expanding the population by this one person will produce a greater sum but a lesser average than the *status quo*. It will therefore be preferred by the classical theory but not by the average theory. It is no accident that the average theory was devised strictly to handle questions of population."

In the modern welfare economics literature, Harsanyi (1953, 1955) and Vickrey (1960) have presented the foundations for utilitarianism in terms of a contractual theory. Since they consider a fixed population, they do not distinguish between classical and average utilitarianism, so that one can view them as advocates of both theories. They envisioned a situation similar to what Rawls (1971) later termed the "original position," which is characterized by a "veil of ignorance." There are two societies (both of size $n$) for you to choose to be in. You know the vector of utility levels that each society has:

$$U^1 = (U^1_1, \ldots, U^1_n) \qquad \text{and} \qquad U^2 = (U^2_1, \ldots, U^2_n).$$

You are denied any information about where in this vector ("in whose shoes") you will be, so you assume that you have an equal probability to be anywhere. If you want to satisfy the von-Neumann-Morgenstern axioms, you will choose the society in which the expected utility ($\sum_{i=1}^{n} U_i^1/n$ or $\sum_{i=1}^{n} U_i^2/n$) is higher. Note that the expected utility in this case is also the average utility. Since $n$ is a constant in the Harsanyi-Vickrey framework, it provides a justification for either classical or average utilitarianism.

If the two societies differ in size, it would seem that the Harsanyi-Vickrey approach still leads to average utilitarianism. As Sumner (1978, p, 100) puts it: "... you will always opt for the higher average; the prospect of larger numbers living at a lower average will hold no attraction for you." However, he also maintains that the Harsanyi-Vickrey approach may well lead to the classical utilitarianism if the framework of the original position is slightly modified. Suppose that the two societies are of different sizes, $n_1$ and $n_2$, and that $n_1 > n_2$. Assume further that the number of the hypothetical contractors (the individuals who are searching for the society to belong to) is known to you and that it is equal to $n_1$. In this case the second society is overbooked and if you choose the second society you will first have to participate in a lottery to determine whether you have a place at all in this society. The probability of having a place is $n_2/n_1$. Therefore, by choosing the first society you obtain an expected utility of $1/n_1 \sum_{i=1}^{n_1} U_i^1$; by choosing the second society you obtain an expected utility of

$$\frac{n_2}{n_1} \frac{1}{n_2} \sum_{i=1}^{n_2} U_i^2 = \frac{1}{n_1} \sum_{i=1}^{n_2} U_i^2.$$

Thus, you will compare $1/n_1 \sum_{i=1}^{n_1} U_i^1$ with $1/n_1 \sum_{i=1}^{n_2} U_i^2$. Eliminating $1/n_1$ yields the sum-of-utilities criterion, or classical utilitarianism.

Some further support for classical utilitarianism may be obtained from the work of Arrow and Kurz (1970). They consider an intergenerational allocation of resources with population changing from one generation to the next (although at an exogenously given rate). The question they address is whether the social welfare function should depend on the average utility in each generation or the total utility in each generation. Arrow and Kurz argue convincingly in favor of the latter criterion.

Suppose that there are two generations of sizes $n_1$ and $n_2$ and an exhaustible resource capable of producing $K$ units of consumption. All members of all generations have the same monotonically increasing and concave utility function $u(\cdot)$. Let $c^i$ be the consumption of each member of generation, $i = 1, 2$.

If the social welfare function depends on the total utility of each generation, $W = W(n_1 u(c^1), n_2 u(c^2))$, the optimal allocation is obtained by solving the following program:

(6.1) $\quad \max_{c^1, c^2} W(n_1 u(c^1), n_2 u(c^2))$, $\quad$ such that $\quad n_1 c^1 + n_2 c^2 \leq K$.

The first-order conditions yield

(6.2a) $$n_1 W_1 u'(c^1) - \lambda n_1 = 0,$$

(6.2b) $$n_2 W_2 u'(c^2) - \lambda n_2 = 0,$$

where $\lambda \geq 0$ is a Lagrange multiplier.

Dividing (6.2a) by (6.2b), one obtains:

(6.3) $$\frac{W_1 u'(c^1)}{W_2 u'(c^2)} = 1.$$

Assuming that $W$ is symmetric (i.e., $W(a, b) = W(b, a)$), it follows from (6.3) that $c^1 = c^2$, so that the social welfare function does not discriminate against any generation.

However, if the social welfare function depends on the average utility of each generation, it will discriminate against the generation with the large population. To see this, one has to solve the following optimization problem:

(6.4) $$\max_{c^1, c^2} W(u(c^1), u(c^2)), \quad \text{such that} \quad n_1 c^1 + n_2 c^2 \leq K.$$

The solution is depicted in Figure 6.1.

By the symmetry of $W$, the slope of the social indifference curve, $W(u(c^1), u(c^2)) = \text{constant}$, is 1 (in absolute value) on the 45° line. The slope of the consumption-possibility frontier, $n_1 c^1 + n_2 c^2 = K$, is $n_1/n_2$ (in absolute value), which is smaller than 1, assuming a positive rate of population growth (i.e., $n_1 < n_2$). Thus, the social optimum must lie to the right of the 45°-line, implying that $c^1 > c^2$. Hence, average utilitarianism discriminates against the generation with the larger population.

Sumner suggests still another argument against average utilitarianism: it gives priority to the existing individuals over potential individuals. Consider, for instance, a society of two individuals, Sue and Ron, having utility levels of 1 and 0, respectively. Suupose that one contemplates adding Gil to the society and transferring the one unit of utility from Sue to him. Classical utilitarianism will be indifferent with respect to this addition since total utility remains 1. However, average utility falls from 1/2 to 1/3, and therefore average utilitarianism will reject the addition of Gil to the society. At the *status quo*, there was one individual (Sue) who had one unit of utility. After the addition, there would also be just one individual (the potential person Gil) with one unit of utility. By rejecting the addition of Gil, average utilitarianism in fact favors the existing person Sue over the potential person Gil.

There are also some objections to classical utilitarianism. Dasgupta (1984), referring to his earlier work (Dasgupta, 1969), points out that "the application of classical utilitarianism in a world with finite resources often implies a

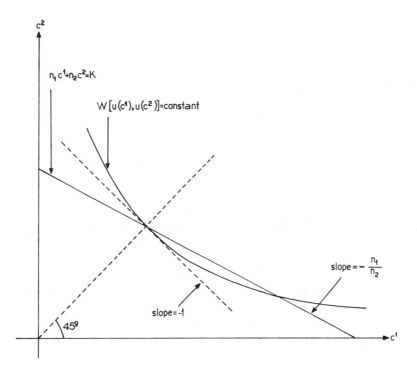

**Figure 6.1.** Socially Optimal Population Size when Social Welfare Depends on the Average Utility of Each Generation.

large population size; by this I mean that the average standard of living is embarrasingly low." As long as the average utility does not fall at too high a rate when population is increasing (i.e., the elasticity of average utility with respect to population size is less than 1 in absolute value), population ought to be increased indefinitely even though the average utility may approach 0.[2] Parfit (1984) calls this "the repugnant conclusion." We deal below with this conclusion when we present our approach to utilitarianism in the presence of endogenous fertility, and we show that classical utilitarianism does not necessarily imply an excessive population size.

## 2.   Individual Choice and Social Optima

Throughout most of this book we use a finite horizon model with endogenous population growth (i.e., endogenous fertility) in which parents care about the number and welfare of their children.[3] By endogenous fertility we mean that parents determine the number of their children who, in turn, determine the number of their children, and so on, so that population size cannot be controlled directly by government or social planners. This does not mean, of course, that a government can have no policy regarding the size of the population, but, rather, that government has to base its population policy on setting the right economic incentives for parents to follow the socially desired population growth path. This means that fertility (parents' decisions about how many children to have) is the endogenous source of population growth.

That parents care about their children's welfare and number is a feature that appears to be absent from other studies of optimal population growth, such as Dasgupta (1969), Lane (1975, 1977), Samuelson (1975), Deardorff (1976), Meade (1976), and others, who assume that population size is determined by society (but see Lane, 1977, pp. 111-119). To the extent that individual preferences are extraneous to fertility determinations, one cannot formulate a laissez-faire solution to the problem of optimal population size, which is the solution that results from utility-maximizing parents in the absence of any government fiats or incentives.

In this section we compare optimal population sizes (or growth rates) for classical utilitarianism (the Benthamite social welfare function) and average utilitarianism (the Millian social welfare function) with each other and with the laissez-faire solution.

Edgeworth (1925) conjectures that the Benthamite criterion leads to a larger population than the Millian criterion. Koopmans (1975), with slightly different versions of the two criteria, makes a similar conjecture. We confirm these conjectures in a more general framework with endogenous fertility: The socially optimal rate of population growth must be larger for a Benthamite than for a Millian social welfare function.[4]

We also find that no unambiguous conclusions can be drawn with respect to the laissez-faire solution in comparison with the socially optimal solution according to either the Benthamite or the Millian criteria. It is not necessarily true that unfettered individual choice will lead to a smaller population than the Benthamite criterion, as Sidgwick thought, or to a larger population than the Millian criterion, as Mill thought.

## 2.a. The Laissez-Faire Allocation

Consider an economy with two generations, each consisting of just one type of consumer. In the first period there is only one adult person. She consumes (together with her children) a single private good ($c^1$). She also raises identical children who grow up in the second period. She dies at the end of the first period, having bequeathed $b$ to each one of her children. The number of children ($n$) that are born in the first period is a decision variable of the parent living then. The number of persons living in the second period is $n$. Each one consumes a single private good $(c^2)$.

The parent's utility includes the children's utilities. In a reduced form we can write the parent's utility as

(6.5)                             $u^1(c^1, n, u^2(c^2))$,

where $u^1$ is concave in $c^1$ and $u^2$, $u^2$ is monotonically increasing and concave in $c^2$, and both $u^1$ and $u^2$ are non-negative (people enjoy positive happiness); $u^1$ is also monotonically increasing in $c^1$ and $u^2$, but it is not monotonic in the number of children $n$. As an example consider the following form:

(6.6a)          $u^1(c^1, n, u^2(c^2)) = v\left(\dfrac{c^1}{(1+n)}, n, nu^2(c^2)\right)$,

where $v$ is monotonically increasing in each one of its three arguments. In this form, the parent's direct utility is $v$, which depends on per capita consumption $(c^1/(1+n))$ of the parent and the children in the first period. The parent may also extract a direct utility from the number of children $(n)$, and she is assumed to care about the total utility $(nu^2)$ of her children in the second period, where the utility of each child $(u^2)$ depends on $c^2$. In this case, $n$ decreases utility (i.e., $u^1$) via $c^1/(1+n)$, increases it directly as the second argument in $v$, and also increases it via $nu^2$. Therefore, $u^1$ need not be monotonic in $n$.

Other possibilities for $u^1$ include

(6.6b)          $u^1(c^1, n, u^2(c^2)) = v\left(\dfrac{c^1}{(1+n)}, n, u^2(c^2)\right)$,

or

(6.6c)          $u^1(c^1, n, u^2(c^2)) = v\left(\dfrac{c^1}{(1+n)}, nu^2(c^2)\right)$,

where, again, $v$ is increasing in each one of its two or three arguments. In (6.6b) the parent's utility depends on the average utility of her children $(u^2)$ rather than the total utility of her children $(nu^2)$. In (6.6c), the parent does not extract a direct utility from the number of her children $(n)$. In these two cases, $u^1$ is also not necessarily monotonic in $n$.

We now turn to the budget constraint facing the parent. She lives only for one period and faces the following budget constraint in this period:

(6.7)                      $c^1 + nb = K$;        $c^1, n \geq 0$,

where $K$ is her initial endowment, which is nonrenewable and does not depreciate over time. This is like having an exhaustible resource capable of producing $K$ units of consumption.

Although we do not restrict the bequest, $b$, to be nonnegative, we show below that it will never be negative. Thus, institutional arrangements that do not allow $b$ to be negative—parents cannot obligate their children to pay their debts—are superfluous here.

Assume that the children are born with no endowments. Thus, the exhaustible resource has to suffice for the consumption of the current and all future generations. The children's per capita consumption is therefore equal to their per capita inheritance:

$$(6.8) \hspace{4cm} c^2 = b.$$

The exact specification of the supply side is not important for the problem of optimal population size *per se* that is considered in this chapter and has no effect on our conclusions with respect to the implications of different social welfare criteria. However, to analyze some problems, such as the relation between population growth and optimal capital accumulation, it is essential to introduce production.[5]

Constraints (6.7)–(6.8) can be consolidated into one budget constraint for the parent:

$$(6.9) \hspace{3cm} c^1 + nc^2 = K; \hspace{1cm} c^1, c^2, n \geq 0.$$

A competitive or laissez-faire allocation (LFA) is obtained when (6.5) is maximized with respect to $c^1$, $c^2$, and $n$, subject to (6.9). Denote this allocation by $(c^{1L}, c^{2L}, n^L)$.

Observe that the feasible set determined by the constraint (6.9) is neither convex nor bounded. The nonboundedness may pose some difficulties. In particular one may let $n$ go to 0 and $c^2$ approach infinity or vice versa. That is, one may opt for as small a number of children as possible and let each one of them enjoy unbounded consumption and vice versa. This means that some restrictions have to be imposed on the utility function to ensure that this course of action does not yield an unbounded utility so that a laissez-faire allocation exists. For example, one may have to restrict a term like $nu^2(c^2)$ to be bounded when $n \to 0$ (and $c^2 \to \infty$). Below we calculate concrete examples of laissez-faire allocations and demonstrate their existence. Similar considerations of boundedness arise with respect to the Benthamite and Millian allocations, discussed below.

## 2.b.   Benthamite and Millian Allocations

In our model the Benthamite social welfare function is defined by

$$(6.10) \hspace{2cm} B(c^1, c^2, n) = u^1(c^1, n, u^2(c^2)) + nu^2(c^2).$$

As mentioned, it is assumed that there is diminishing marginal utility of $c^1$ and $c^2$, i.e., $u^1_{11}, u^2_{11} < 0$, where subscripts stand for partial derivatives. A

Bentham optimal allocation (BOA) is obtained by maximizing (6.10) with respect to $c^1$, $c^2$ and $n$, subject to (6.9). Denote this allocation by $(c^{1B}, c^{2B}, n^B)$.

The Millian social welfare function in our model is defined by

$$(6.11) \qquad M(c^1, c^2, n) = \frac{u^1(c^1, n, u^2(c^2)) + nu^2(c^2)}{1 + n} = \frac{B(c^1, c^2, n)}{1 + n}.$$

The Millian optimal allocation (MOA) is obtained by maximizing (6.11) with respect to $c^1$, $c^2$, and $n$, subject to the resource constraint (6.9). Denote this allocation by $(c^{1M}, c^{2M}, n^M)$.

It is important to emphasize that we assume that the parent's utility function represents her *interest* (e.g., happiness from being a parent, relief in providing for the children, etc.) rather than her *moral* (social) preferences (e.g., believing that it would be wrong to have children and let them starve). This is why we add $nu^2(c^2)$ to $u^1(c^1, n, u^2(c^2))$ when we define our Benthamite and Millian social welfare criteria; if we were to adopt the second interpretation, that parents get no happiness at all from caring for their children, adding $nu^2(c^2)$ to $u^1(c^1, n, u^2(c^2))$ would be superfluous. In that case, however, we would not have a theory of *endogenous* fertility, which lies at the heart of this book.

### 2.c. A Comparison of Population Sizes

In this section we show that when fertility is endogenous, although the Benthamite social welfare criterion always leads to a larger population than the Millian, the laissez-faire allocation may lead to a larger or smaller population size, that is, that the population size in the LFA may be higher than that in the BOA or lower than that in the MOA.

#### 2.c.1. Comparison Between the BOA and the MOA. 
Observe that both the BOA and the MOA satisfy the same resource constraint, (6.9). Since the Millian allocation maximizes $M$ and since $M = B/(1 + n)$, it follows that

$$(6.12) \qquad \frac{B(c^{1M}, c^{2M}, n^M)}{1 + n^M} \geq \frac{B(c^{1B}, c^{2B}, n^B)}{1 + n^B}.$$

Since $(c^{1B}, c^{2B}, n^B)$ maximizes $B$, it follows that

$$(6.13) \qquad B(c^{1B}, c^{2B}, n^B) \geq B(c^{1M}, c^{2M}, c^M).$$

Therefore,

$$\frac{1 + n^M}{1 + n^B} \leq \frac{B(c^{1M}, c^{2M}, n^M)}{B(c^{1B}, c^{2B}, n^B)} \leq 1,$$

from which it follows that $n^B \geq n^M$.[6]

**2.c.2.   A comparison Between the MOA and the LFA.**   Since the Millian criterion calls for a maximization of the average utility, intuition suggests that laissez-faire results in overpopulation. Although this may be true, however, under some circumstances, it does not hold in general.

Since the LFA satisfied the same resource constraint, (6.9), as does the MOA, it follows from the very definition of the MOA that

$$(6.14) \qquad M(c^{1M}, c^{2M}, n^M) \geq M(c^{1L}, c^{2L}, n^L).$$

Since $M = B/(1 + n)$, it is implied by (6.14) that

$$(6.15) \qquad B(c^{1M}, c^{2M}, n^M) \geq \left(\frac{1 + n^M}{1 + n^L}\right) B(c^{1L}, c^{2L}, n^L).$$

Since $u^2 \geq 0$, it also follows that

$$
\begin{aligned}
B(c^{1L}, c^{2L}, n^L) &= u^1(c^{1L}, n^L, u^2(c^{2L})) + n^L u^2(c^{2L}) \\
&\geq u^1(c^{1L}, n^L, u^2(c^{2L})) \\
&\geq u^1(c^{1M}, n^M, u^2(c^{2M})),
\end{aligned}
$$

(6.16)

because $(c^{1L}, c^{2L}, n^L)$ maximizes $u^1$ subject to the overall resource constraint (6.9). Thus, we conclude from (6.15) and (6.16) that

$$B(c^{1M}, c^{2M}, n^M) \geq \left(\frac{1 + n^M}{1 + n^L}\right) u^1(c^{1M}, n^M, u^2(c^{2M})),$$

so that

$$(6.17) \qquad
\begin{aligned}
\frac{1 + n^M}{1 + n^L} &\leq \frac{B(c^{1M}, c^{2M}, n^M)}{u^1(c^{1M}, n^M, u^2(c^{2M}))} \\
&= \frac{u^1(c^{1M}, n^M, u^2(c^{2M})) + n^M u^2(c^{2M})}{u^1(c^{1M}, n^M, u^2(c^{2M}))} \\
&= 1 + \frac{n^M u^2(c^{2M})}{u^1(c^{1M}, n^M, u^2(c^{2M}))}.
\end{aligned}
$$

Since the extreme right-hand side of (6.17) is strictly greater than 1, it is impossible to say anything about the ratio on the extreme left-hand side, in particular, one cannot conclude that $n^L \geq n^M$.

Indeed, in the example that follows we show that the population size in the MOA can bear any relationship to the population size in the LFA. In particular, the LFA could result in an underpopulated world relative to the MOA.

*Example.* Let the parent's utility function be

(6.18)    $u^1(c^1, n, u^2(c^2)) = c^1 + an - \frac{1}{2}gn^2 + nu^2(c^2),$    $a, g > 0,$

where $u^2(c^2) = \log(1 + c^2)$.

The Millian criterion in this case is

(6.19)    $$\frac{u^1 + nu^2}{1 + n} = \frac{c^1 + an - \frac{1}{2}gn^2 + 2n\log(1 + c^2)}{1 + n}.$$

In order to find the MOA, substitute the resource constraint $c^1 = K - nc^2$ into (6.19) which becomes

(6.20)    $$\frac{an - \frac{1}{2}gn^2 + K + n[2\log(1 + c^2) - c^2]}{1 + n}.$$

In order to find the MOA, maximize (6.20) with respect to $c^2$ and $n$, subject to the constraint $nc^2 \leq K$ (so that $c^1 \geq 0$). Clearly, $c^{2M}$ must maximize

$$2\log(1 + c^2) - c^2.$$

Hence, we conclude that $c^{2M} = 1$. Substituting this into (6.20), we can also conclude that $n^M$ must maximize

$$\frac{an - \frac{1}{2}gn^2 + K + n[2\log 2 - 1]}{1 + n}.$$

Hence,

(6.21)    $$n^M = \frac{-g + [g^2 + 2ag + 4g\log 2 - 2g(1 + K)]^{1/2}}{g}.$$

We also have $c^{1M} = K - n^M c^{2M} = K - n^M$ (because $c^{2M} = 1$).

The LFA is found by maximizing

(6.22)    $$K - nc^2 + an - \frac{1}{2}gn^2 + n\log(1 + c^2)$$
$$= K + an - \frac{1}{2}gn^2 + n[\log(1 + c^2) - c^2]$$

with respect to $n$ and $c^2$. Clearly, $c^{2L}$ must maximize

$$\log(1 + c^2) - c^2,$$

and, hence, we conclude that $c^{2L} = 0$. Substituting this into (6.22), it is evident that $n^L$ must maximize

$$K + an - \frac{1}{2}gn^2.$$

Hence,

(6.23) $$n^L = \frac{a}{g},$$

and we also have $c^{1L} = K - n^L c^{2L} = K$.

Comparing (6.21) with (6.23),

(6.24) $$n^L \gtreqless n^M \quad \text{according as}$$

$$\frac{a}{g} \gtreqless \frac{-g + [g^2 + 2ag + 4g \log 2 - 2g(1 + K)]^{1/2}}{g}.$$

With some simplifications, (6.24) reduces to

$$n^L \gtreqless n^M \text{ according as } a^2 \gtreqless 4g \log 2 - 2g(1 + K).$$

Thus, depending on $a$, $g$, and $K$, the Millian population size can be greater than, equal to, or smaller than the laissez-faire population size.

### 2.c.3. Comparison Between the BOA and the LFA.

Since the Benthamite criterion calls for a maximization of total utility of parents and children, while the competitive allocation maximizes the parent's utility only, intuition suggests that laissez-faire leads to a smaller than socially optimal population. However, this is not necessarily true: when $nu^2(c^2)$ is added to the parent's utility, as suggested by the Benthamite criterion, increasing the product $nu^2(c^2)$ is indeed desirable, but it does not follow that both $n$ and $c^2$ have to be increased.

To see this, observe that it follows from the definition of the LFA and the BOA that

$$u^1(c^{1L}, n^L, u^2(c^{2L})) \geq u^1(c^{1B}, n^B, u^2(c^{2B})),$$

and

$$u^1(c^{1B}, n^B, u^2(c^{2B})) + n^B u^2(c^{2B}) \geq u^1(c^{1L}, n^L, u^2(c^{2L})) + n^L u^2(c^{2L}).$$

Hence,

$$n^B u^2(c^{2B}) \geq n^L u^2(c^{2L}).$$

Thus, the total utility from children ($nu^2$) must be larger in the BOA than in the LFA.

However, as we noted above, increasing $nu^2(c^2)$ does not necessarily imply increases of both $n$ and $c^2$, because, as explained in Chapter 5, raising either $n$ or $c^2$ raises the "price" of the other in the resource constraint, (6.9). Indeed, in the example that follows, $c^{2B} > c^{2L}$, but the relation between $n^B$ and $n^L$ is ambiguous and, depending on the parameter values, it is possible that $n^B < n^L$.

*Example.* Let the parent's utility function be

(6.25) $$u^1(c^1, n, u^2(c^2)) = nc^1 - n^2 + nu^2(c^2),$$

where

$$u^2(c^2) = a \log(1 + c^2), \qquad a > 0.$$

Substituting $c^1 = K - nc^2$ into (6.26), the LFA can be found by maximizing

(6.26) $$n(K - nc^2) - n^2 + an \log(1 + c^2)$$

with respect to $n$ and $c^2$. The first-order conditions are

(6.27) $$K + a \log(1 + c^{2L}) - 2n^L(1 + c^{2L}) = 0$$

and

(6.28) $$-n^L + \frac{a}{1 + c^{2L}} = 0,$$

from which it follows that

(6.29) $$n^L(1 + c^{2L}) = a.$$

Hence, (6.27) becomes

$$K + a \log(1 + c^{2L}) - 2a = 0,$$

which yields

(6.30) $$\log(1 + c^{2L}) = 2 - K/a.^7$$

Taking the logarithms of both sides of (6.29) yields

(6.31) $$\log n^L + \log(1 + c^{2L}) = \log a.$$

Substituting (6.30) into (6.31),

(6.32) $$\log n^L = \log a + K/a - 2.$$

The BOA is achieved by maximizing

(6.26') $$n(K - nc^2) - n^2 + 2an \log(1 + c^2)$$

with respect to $n$ and $c^2$. Comparing (6.26) with (6.26'), one sees that the latter differs from the former only by one term: $2a$ replaces $a$. Hence, the solutions for $c^{2B}$ and $n^B$ are obtained by substituting $2a$ for $a$ in (6.30) and (6.32):

(6.30') $$\log(1 + c^{2B}) = 2 - K/2a,$$

and

(6.32')                    $\log n^b = \log(2a) + K/2a - 2.$

Comparing (6.30') with (6.30), one can indeed see that $c^{2L} < c^{2B}$, namely, the BOA grants children more consumption than does the LFA. However, depending on the parameter values ($K$ and $a$), it may be that $n^B < n^L$. To see this, note from (6.32') and (6.32) that $n^B < n^L$ if and only if $\log(2a) + K/2a - 2 < \log a + K/a - 2$. Thus, $n^B < n^L$ if and only if $\log 4 < K/a$. Obviously, one can choose $K$ and $a$ in such a way that $\log 4 < K/a$, so that $n^B < n^L$: the Benthamite population size is smaller than the laissez-faire population size.[8]

### 3.   Optimal Population Policies

In this section we analyze policy interventions that may be necessary to support the population sizes and consumptions that are socially optimal according to the Millian and Benthamite criteria. These are noncoercive (price-based) policies aimed at moving an economy from the unfettered LFA to either the BOA or the MOA. This approach has an advantage over that taken in existing literature on optimum population: In that literature the only population policy the government can use is a coercive one; the fertility rate is determined by fiat. In our approach, parents determine fertility, and the government can influence fertility decisions only by an appropriate set of economic or market incentives.

We consider all possible direct and indirect taxes and subsidies as candidates for policy interventions. Note that in our case children themselves are a commodity and may be subject to a tax or a subsidy. Such a head tax is *not* a lump-sum nondistortionary tax as in the traditional economic literature with exogenous population. This tax affects fertility decisions on the margin.

Among the set of possible direct and indirect taxes and subsidies to achieve a social optimum, we find that it is necessary to use interest rate subsidies (to encourage future consumption) and child allowances (positive or negative to encourage or discourage having children). We show that an interest rate subsidy is warranted under both the Benthamite and the Millian criteria; a positive child allowance is necessary under the Benthamite criterion but the child allowance needed under the Millian criterion may be positive, zero, or negative. It should be emphasized that these policies are *first-best* policies in that they actually achieve the BOA and the MOA. This is to be distinguished from second-best policies which are the best policies *towards* approximating the Benthamite or the Millian goals but do not actually achieve one or the other.

### 3.a.   A Benthamite Incentive Policy

Consider first the BOA. It is obtained by maximizing

$$u^1(c^1, n, u^2(c^2)) + nu^2(c^2),$$

subject to the resource constraint:

$$K - c^1 - nc^2 = 0$$

(see (6.10) and (6.9) above).

Letting $\lambda \geq 0$ be the Lagrange multiplier, one derives the following first-order conditions for an interior solution:

(6.33a)                          $u_1^1 = \lambda,$

(6.33b)                          $u_2^1 + u^2 = \lambda c^2,$

(6.33c)                          $u_3^1 u_1^2 + nu_1^2 = \lambda n.$

Dividing (6.33b) and (6.33c) by (6.33a), one obtains

(6.34a)                          $\dfrac{u_2^1 + u^2}{u_1^1} = c^2,$

(6.34b)                          $\dfrac{u_3^1 u_1^2 + nu_1^2}{u_1^1} = n.$

Equation (6.34a) asserts that the *social* marginal rate of substitution of $c^1$ for $n$ (the willingness of society to give up a parent's consumption for an additional child, which is $(u_2^1 + u^2)/u_1^1$), must be equated to the *social* "cost" of an additional child, which is equal to its consumption, $c^2$. Similarly, equation (6.34b) asserts that the *social* marginal rate of substitution of $c^1$ for $c^2$ must be equated to the *social* "cost" of a unit of the child's consumption, which is $n$, since every one of the $n$ children consumes this unit.

In order to achieve the BOA allocation (via the market mechanism), it may be possible for the government to subsidize $c^2$ at the rate of $\alpha$ (for example, by subsidizing the interest rate, which is implicitly assumed here to be 0), to give child allowances (possibly negative) of $\beta$ per child, and to balance its budget by a lump-sum tax (possibly negative) in the amount $T$. In this case the parent's budget constraint becomes

(6.35)                  $c^1 + nc^2(1 - \alpha) = K + \beta n - T.$

Given this budget constraint, the parent maximizes

$$u^1(c^1, n, u^2(c^2))$$

by choosing $c^1$, $n$, and $c^2$ (see (6.5) above). Letting $\theta \geq 0$ be the Lagrange multiplier for this problem, one obtains the following first-order conditions for an interior solution:

(6.36a) $$u_1^1 = \theta,$$

(6.36b) $$u_2^1 = -\theta\beta + \theta c^2(1 - \alpha),$$

(6.36c) $$u_3^1 u_1^2 = \theta n(1 - \alpha).$$

Dividing (6.36b) and (6.36c) by (6.36a), one obtains:

(6.37a) $$\frac{u_2^1}{u_1^1} = c^2(1 - \alpha) - \beta,$$

(6.37b) $$\frac{u_3^1 u_1^2}{u_1^1} = n(1 - \alpha).$$

Equation (6.37a) states that the marginal rate of substitution of $c^1$ for $n$ (i.e., a parent's willingness to give up her own consumption for an additional child) must be equated to the "price" of a child, as perceived by the parent from the budget constraint (6.35). The "price" consists of two components: the cost of providing the child with $c^2$ units of consumption, which is only $c^2(1 - \alpha)$ due to the subsidy $\alpha$, and the tax on children, which is $-\beta$. Equation (6.37b) states that the marginal rate of substitution of $c^1$ for $c^2$ must be equated to the "price" of $c^2$, which is the number of children times $1 - \alpha$.

To achieve a BOA in this way, one finds the optimal level of $\alpha$ and $\beta$ by comparing the first-order conditions for the BOA (namely, (6.34)) with those of the parent's optimization problem (6.37). First, compare (6.34b) with (6.37b) to conclude that

$$n(1 - \alpha) = n\left(1 - \frac{u_1^2}{u_1^1}\right),$$

so that the optimal subsidy to children's consumption under the Benthamite criterion is

(6.38) $$\alpha^B = \frac{u_1^2(c^{1B}, n^B, u^2(c^{2B}))}{u_1^1(c^{1B}, n^B, u^2(c^{2B}))}.$$

Next, compare (6.36a) with (6.37a) to conclude that

$$c^2 - \frac{u^2}{u_1^1} = c^2(1 - \alpha) - \beta,$$

so that the optimal child allowance under the Benthamite criterion is

(6.39) $$\beta^B = \frac{u^2(c^{2B})}{u_1^1(c^{1B}, n^B, u^2(c^{2B}))} - \alpha^B c^{2B}.$$

Notice that $\alpha$ and $\beta$ play the role of a Pigouvian tax or subsidy. Since the term $nu^2(c^2)$ of the Benthamite criterion (6.10) is ignored in the parent's utility (6.5), in this case $c^2$ generates an external economy from a social point of view; hence, it ought to be subsidized in order to achieve the BOA. The optimal magnitude of this subsidy has to be determined according to what the parent ignores (at the margin). When the parent considers increasing $c^2$, she ignores the social benefit $nu_1^2$ at the margin. This benefit is measured in utility units. Its equivalent in terms of the numeraire consumption good is $nu_1^2/u_1^1$. From the parent's budget constraint (6.35), one can see that if $c^2$ is subsidized at the rate $\alpha$, then each unit of $c^2$ receives a subsidy of $n\alpha$. Thus, the Pigouvian subsidy ought to be set at a level such that $n\alpha = nu_1^2/u_1^1$, which explains the magnitude of the optimal $\alpha$ in (6.38).

For the same reason, $n$ ought to be subsidized by $u^2/u_1^1$ so that the price of $n$ for the parent will be $c^2 - (u^2/u_1^1)$. Since, by the parent's budget constraint (6.35), the price of $n$ is $c^2(1 - \alpha) - \beta$, $c^2 - (u^2/u_1^1)$ is equated to $c^2(1 - \alpha) - \beta$. Thus, it follows that $\beta^B = (u^2/u_1^1) - \alpha^B c^2$, as in (6.39).

Note that $\alpha^B > 0$ and can be implemented by a subsidy to the rate of interest (assumed to be 0 in this model). To find the sign of $\beta^B$, observe that

$$\beta^B = \frac{u^2}{u_1^1} - \alpha^B c^2 = \frac{u^2 - c^2 u_1^2}{u_1^1}$$

by substituting (6.38) into (6.39). Since $u^2$ is concave, it follows that

$$u^2(c^2) - u^2(0) \geq u_1^2(c^2)(c^2 - 0).$$

Since $u^2$ is assumed to be nonnegative, it follows that

$$u^2(c^2) \geq c^2 u_1^2(c^2),$$

so that $\beta^B > 0$: The optimal child allowance under the Benthamite criterion must be positive.

Fixed $\alpha$ and $\beta$ may not in fact lead to the BOA because the parent's optimization problem is not convex; therefore, the second-order conditions may not hold. If the second-order conditions do not hold with fixed $\alpha$ and $\beta$, it is possible to achieve a BOA with nonlinear taxes, i.e., with instruments $\alpha$ and $\beta$ that are functions of $c^1$, $c^2$, and $n$. In other words, one can always satisfy the second-order conditions by functions $\alpha(\cdot)$ and $\beta(\cdot)$.[9] The values of $\alpha(\cdot)$ and $\beta(\cdot)$ at the optimum will be exactly $\alpha^B$ and $\beta^B$ as given in (6.38) and (6.39), i.e.,

$$\alpha^B = \alpha(c^{1B}, n^B, c^{2B}),$$

and

$$\beta^B = \beta(c^{1B}, n^B, c^{2B}).$$

### 3.b.    A Millian Incentive Policy

We now turn to the MOA. This allocation is obtained by maximizing

$$\frac{u^1(c^1, n, u^2(c^2)) + nu^2(c^2)}{1 + n},$$

subject to the resource constraint

$$K - c^1 - nc^2 \leq 0$$

(see (6.11) and (6.9) above).

Letting $\lambda \geq 0$ be the Lagrange multiplier for this optimization problem, one derives the following first-order conditions for an interior solution:

$$(6.40a) \qquad\qquad\qquad\qquad \frac{u_1^1}{1 + n} = \lambda,$$

$$(6.40b) \qquad\qquad \frac{(u_2^1 + u^2)(1 + n) - u^1 - nu^2}{(1 + n)^2} = \lambda c^2,$$

$$(6.40c) \qquad\qquad\qquad \frac{u_3^1 u_1^2 + nu_1^2}{1 + n} = \lambda n.$$

Dividing (6.40b) and (6.40c) by (6.40a), one obtains:

$$(6.41a) \qquad\qquad \frac{u_2^1 + u^2}{u_1^1} - \frac{u^1 + nu^2}{(1 + n)u_1^1} = c^2,$$

$$(6.41b) \qquad\qquad\qquad \frac{u_3^1 u_1^2}{u_1^1} + n\frac{u_1^2}{u_1^1} = n.$$

These two equations have a similar interpretation to equations (6.34a) and (6.34b) in terms of equating social marginal rates of substitution to social marginal costs. Following the procedure of the preceding subsection, we compare (6.41a) and (6.41b) with the first-order conditions (6.37a) and (6.37b) for the parent's optimization problem in order to find the optimal $\alpha$ and $\beta$ for the Millian criterion. First, compare (6.41b) with (6.37b) to conclude that

$$(6.42) \qquad\qquad\qquad \alpha^M = \frac{u_1^2(c^{2M})}{u_1^1(c^{1M}, n^M, u^2(c^{2M}))}.$$

Next, compare (6.41a) with (6.37a) to conclude that

$$c^2(1 - \alpha) - \beta = c^2 + \frac{u^1 + nu^2}{(1 + n)u_1^1} - \frac{u^2}{u_1^1}.$$

Hence,

$$(6.43) \qquad \beta^M = \frac{u^2(c^{2M})}{u_1^1(c^{1M}, n^M, u^2(c^{2M}))} - \alpha^M c^{2M}$$
$$- \frac{u^1(c^{1M}, n^M, u^2(c^{2M})) + n^M u^2(c^{2M})}{(1 + n^M)u^1(c^{1M}, n^M, u^2(c^{2M}))}.$$

These formulae for the optimal $\alpha$ and $\beta$ under the Millian criterion could be given a similar interpretation of Pigouvian taxes or subsidies as we did for the Benthamite criterion (formulae (6.38) and (6.39)).[10] The subsidy to child consumption, namely $\alpha^M$, is positive, as in the Benthamite case. But the sign of the optimal child allowance ($\beta^M$) is ambiguous in this case. The reason for this ambiguity can be seen by comparing the Millian social welfare, which is $(u^1 + nu^2)/(1 + n)$, with the parent's utility, which is just $u^1$. On one hand, the Millian function adds $nu^2$ to the parent's function, and in this way $n$ generates a positive externality; on the other hand, $u^1 + nu^2$ is also divided by $(1 + n)$, and in this way $n$ generates a negative externality. Thus, one cannot determine a priori whether $n$ should be taxed or subsidized.

## 4. An Infinite Horizon Model

In this section we attempt to analyze some of the issues raised in the preceding sections in an infinite horizon setting. In particular, we reconsider the comparison between Bentham and Mill. A literal extension of the Benthamite social welfare function to an infinite horizon setting when population is endogenous is impractical because the total sum of utilities of infinitely many generations may be unbounded. Hence, we attempt a somewhat indirect approach applicable to steady-state comparisons.

We consider a simple family utility function in which consumption, number of children, and the per capita welfare of children enter as arguments. Each family is assumed to live for two periods, once as children and once as adults. Each generation receives an endowment, $K$, per capita, which may be consumed only in the second period of life; in the first period of life, children consume only what their parents give them. Along a stationary path there are no bequests other than those implicit in the provision of parents for children in the first period.

The Millian stationary path is the one that maximizes, over all possible stationary paths, the per capita welfare, which is nothing else but the infinite-horizon utility of a representative parent.

The Benthamite stationary path is defined here as the one that maximizes, over all possible stationary paths, the sum of infinite-horizon utilities of two adjacent generations in a representative family. In other words, this path maximizes the sum of the welfare of a representative parent plus the total welfare of her or his immediate offspring.

Let $c^1$ and $c^2$ be the consumption of parents and children, respectively. The infinite-horizon utility of a representative parent is

$$(6.44) \qquad\qquad W = \max_{c^1, c^2, n} W^*(c^1, c^2, n, W),$$

subject to

$$(6.45) \qquad\qquad c^1 + nc^2 = K,$$

where $W^*$ is an intertemporal welfare evaluator (see Koopmans et al., 1964). Welfare, $W$, is defined implicitly in this formulation of the problem. We assume that $W^*$ is linearly separable, $W^*(c^1, c^2, n, W) = u(c^1, c^2, n) + \delta W$, where $0 < \delta < 1$ is a subjective intergenerational discount factor. The maximand in the above problem, therefore, reduces to

$$(6.46) \qquad\qquad u(c^1, c^2, n).$$

Thus, the Millian path maximizes (6.46) subject to the resource constraint (6.45), and the Benthamite path maximizes

$$(6.47) \qquad\qquad (1 + n)u(c^1, c^2, n),$$

subject to the same resource constraint, (6.45).

Let $(c^{1M}, c^{2M}, n^M)$ and $(c^{1B}, c^{2B}, n^B)$ be the Millian and Bentham stationary allocations, respectively. Then, in the same manner as in Section 1, one can show that $n^B > n^M$, i.e., the population growth rate is higher under the Bentham criterion than under the Millian one.[11]


## 5. Conclusion

This chapter has considered two social welfare criteria for optimal population size in a simple two-generation model: average utility (Millian criterion) and total utility (Benthamite criterion). We compare the outcome under the two criteria with each other and with the laissez-faire solution and find that although the optimal size from a Benthamite point of view always exceeds that from a Millian, the laissez-faire solution may lie on either side. The conclusion is not altered in the infinite-generation case provided one compares only stationary population growth paths.


## Notes

1.    Sumner (1978, p. 107) maintains that average utilitarianism is incorrectly attributed to Mill. He writes that "... it seems to have originated early in this century among welfare economists." See Chapter 1, especially Note 2, for a discussion of this controversy.

2. Consider the following example: $u(c) = c^{\alpha}$, where $0 < \alpha < 1$. There is an exhaustible resource capable of producing $K$ units of consumption. If the population size is $n$, average utility is $(K/n)^{\alpha}$, and total utility is $K^{\alpha}n^{1-\alpha}$, which approaches infinity as population size approaches infinity. Thus, population ought to be increased indefinitely even though average utility, $(K/n)^{\alpha}$, approaches zero.

3. An extension to an infinite horizon is considered in Section 3 of this chapter.

4. The relation between the Benthamite and the Millian social welfare functions was also considered in the famous debate between Samuelson (1958 and 1959) and Lerner (1959a and 1959b). The focus there, however, was on optimal capital accumulation (or savings) when population growth is exogenous; see also Lane (1975), who discusses this issue in some detail.

5. Although there is no production in our model, capital for bequests here is a form of "capital" passed on from parents to children.

6. This proof is due to T. N. Srinivasan and is much shorter and more elegant than our original proof.

7. In order to ensure that $c^{2L} > 0$, or, equivalently, $\log(1 + c^{2L}) > 0$, it is required that $K/a < 2$.

8. Observe that the condition that $K/a > \log 4$ is consistent with the earlier restriction that $K/a < 2$, because $2 > \log 4$.

9. The nonconvexity appears both in the utility function and in the budget constraint. Moreover, the nonconvexity of the utility function cannot be remedied by transformation because this function is cardinally defined under both classical and average utilitarianism.

10. Notice that here again a nonlinear tax instrument may be required, i.e., $\alpha$ and $\beta$ as *functions* of $c^1$, $n$, and $c^2$, in order to support the MOA.

11. Steady-state comparisons are not always meaningful since they ignore the transition to the steady state. Our present analysis suffers from the same weakness. The more difficult problem of comparing growth rates of a population under alternative utilitarianism criteria in a dynamic infinite horizon model is left for future research.

# References

Arrow, K. J. and M. Kurz (1970), *Public Investment, the Rate of Return and Optimal Fiscal Policy.* Baltimore: Johns Hopkins Press.

Dasgupta, Partha (1969), "On the Concept of Optimum Population," *Review of Economic Studies*, **36**, 295–318.

Dasgupta, Partha (1984), "Ethical Foundations of Population Policies," Paper prepared for the Committee on Population National Research Council, Washington, D. C..

Deardoff, A. V. (1976), "The Growth Rate of Population: Comment," *International Economic Review*, **17**, 510–15.

Edgeworth, F. Y. (1925), Review of Henry Sidgewick's *The Elements of Politics*, in *Papers Relating to Political Economy*, Vol. III, pp. 15–20. London: Macmillan and Company.

Harsanyi, J. C. (1953), "Cardinal Utility in Welfare Economics and in the Theory of Risk Taking," *Journal of Political Economy*, **61**, 434–5.

Harsanyi, J. C. (1955), "Cardinal Welfare, Individualistic Ethics, and Interpersonal Comparisons of Utility," *Journal of Political Economy*, **63**, 309–21.

Koopmans, Tjalling C. (1975), "Concepts of Optimality and Their Uses." Nobel Memorial Prize Lecture, Royal Swedish Academy of Sciences. Stockholm, December 11.

Koopmans, Tjalling C., Peter A. Diamond, and R. A. Williamson (1964), "Stationary Utility and Time Perspective," *Econometrica*, **32**, 82–100.

Lane, John S. (1975), "A Synthesis of the Ramsey-Meade Problems when Population Change is Endogenous," *Review of Economic Studies*, **42**, 57–66.

Lane, John S. (1977), *On Optimal Population Paths*. Berlin: Springer-Verlag.

Lerner, A. P. (1959a), "Consumption-Loan Interest and Money," *Journal of Political Economy*, **67**, 512–8.

Lerner, A. P. (1959b), "Rejoinder," *Journal of Political Economy*, **67**, 523–5.

Meade, J. E. (1976), *The Just Economy*. London: Allen and Unwin.

Parfit, D. (1984), *Reasons and Persons*. Oxford: Oxford University Press.

Rawls, John (1971), *A Theory of Justice*. Cambridge: Harvard University Press.

Samuelson, P. A. (1958), "An Exact Consumption-Loan Model of Interest with or without the Social Contrivance of Money," *Journal of Political Economy*, **66**, 467–82.

Samuelson, P. A. (1959), "Reply," *Journal of Political Economy*, **67**, 518–22.

Samuelson, P. A. (1975), "The Optimum Growth Rate for Population," *International Economic Review*, **16**, 531–38.

Sumner, L. W. (1978), "Classical Utilitarianism and Population Optimum," in R. I. Sikora and Brian Barry (eds.), *Obligations to Future Generations*. Philadelphia: Temple University Press.

Vickrey, W. (1980), "Utility, Strategy and Social Decision Rules," *Quarterly Journal of Economics*, **74**, 507–35.

CHAPTER 7

# Potential Market Failures

In this and the next chapter we consider several potential sources of externalities and market failure in relation to population size and intergenerational allocation of resources. After scrutiny some of these potential sources of market failure prove to be nonexistent; they are considered in this chapter. Other potential sources of externalities prove to be real and require corrective policies; they are discussed in the next chapter.

One has to be careful here about how one characterizes a situation of market failure that calls for corrective government action in the form of taxation. In the preceding chapter we demonstrated the need for a policy intervention in order to attain certain social optima (the Benthamite and the Millian optima). But failure to achieve such optima does not necessarily imply a market failure. The need for a corrective policy in those cases arose because the society had a different set of values (see eq. (6.10) or (6.11)) than that of the parent (the objective function, eq. (6.5)). But the laissez-faire allocation was the best allocation for the parent alive at the time the decision on the allocation of resources and population size was made. Had society adopted the parent's objective, no corrective government action would have been needed. Therefore, we do not characterize the situations of the preceding

81

chapter as market failures. When we ask here whether or not a market failure exists, we are asking whether the laissez-faire allocation attained in the market is the best allocation from the point of view of the parent.

We emphasize again that this notion of market failure in relation to population size is unique to our approach; the laissez-faire allocation has no meaning unless fertility is endogenous. In particular, this concept of market failure cannot be considered in traditional economic models in which fertility is exogenous to the individual decision makers because in such models the notion of laissez-faire population size has no meaning.

We consider three potential causes of market failure. First, if there are *pure* public goods—such as national defense, basic research, weather forecasts, etc.—the per capita costs of providing these goods fall as population size increases. Since everyone enjoys these goods at no additional cost, it is possible that there exists a market failure in relation to population size resulting in the inefficiency of laissez-faire. Second, a fixed resource, such as land, which must be combined with labor to produce goods for consumption, could lead to Malthusian diminishing returns to larger population size. This situation suggests a potential source of external diseconomies and market failure in relation to population size.[1] Third, there is the problem associated with the infinity of generations in an overlapping generation model. In his seminal paper, Samuelson (1958) showed that even without the standard sources of market failure (externalities and nonconvexities), the competitive equilibrium may fail to achieve Pareto efficiency.

In this chapter we show that when fertility is endogenous, these potential sources of market failure do not exist: laissez-faire policy leads individual decision makers to a Pareto-optimal allocation from their point of view.

## 1. Public Goods and Malthusian Fixed Land

In reviewing Sidgewick's *The Elements of Politics*, Edgeworth (1925, p. 20) alludes to the prevailing view among eminent writers that the desirability of large population should not only be sought as an end by itself, but also "for the sake of defense against or competition with foreign nations." These considerations "have perhaps the first claim on the attention of the statesman; being must be secured before well-being." Putting it in a more modern language, a larger population has an advantage in providing *pure* public goods (e.g., national defense, basic research, etc.) because the per capita cost of providing a public good falls as the population becomes larger.[2] This consideration suggests the possibility of market failure: laissez-faire decisions concerning childbearing might lead to underpopulation.

On the other hand, the Malthusian worry about the diminishing marginal (as well as average) productivity of labor, given a fixed amount of land, appears to imply an external diseconomy that has the opposite effect on the optimal population size. Malthus suggested that population will increase whenever the wage is higher than a minimum-subsistence wage and that therefore, in the long run, the wage tends to fall to its minimum-subsistence level. In the Malthusian view, each parent is atomistically small and therefore treats the wage as independent of reproduction decisions. Such perception is indeed true for each individual separately, but not for the society as a whole, and so there might be a market failure leading to overpopulation.

In this section we examine these two issues relating to population growth. As always, we assume that parents care both about the number and the well-being of their offspring. In such a context we show that, surprisingly, these two possible externalities do not actually lead to market failures: the potential externalities are properly internalized within the family, and a competitive equilibrium is Pareto efficient from the standpoint of the present generation. To show this, let us consider, for the sake of simplicity, a two-period model with one parent in the first period. (An extension to infinite horizon is contained in the appendix to this chapter.)

The fixed endowment $K$ of Chapter 6 is replaced here by a fixed resource, land, and fixed supply of labor per capita (i.e., there are no labor-leisure decisions). Land is used in each period together with labor to produce a single good that can be used as private consumption ($c^i$) and public consumption ($P^i$) in period $i = 1, 2$. Due to the Malthusian fixed factor (land), there is a diminishing marginal product of labor. Assuming that the labor endowment is one unit, output is $f(1)$ in the first period. The parent in the first period bears $n$ children. Therefore, output is $f(n)$ in the second period. We assume that $f' > 0$ and $f'' < 0$.

The consumption possibilities of this economy can be described by the following two resource constraints:

(7.1) $$c^1 + P^1 + b = f(1),$$

and

(7.2) $$nc^2 + P^2 = b + f(n),$$

where $b$ is the quantity of consumption transferred from the parent in the first period to her children in the second period.[3] Constraint (7.2) implicitly assumes that consumption can be stored from the first to the second period without "wear and tear." These two constraints can be combined to yield a single constraint:

(7.3) $$c^1 + nc^2 + P^1 + p^2 = f(1) + f(n).$$

A competitive profit-maximization implies that

(7.4)   $w^1 = f'(1)$, $w^2 = f'(n)$, $\Pi^1 = f(1) - f'(1)$, and $\Pi^2 = f(n) - nf'(n)$,

where $w^i$ is the market wage rate and $\Pi^i$ is the land rent (profit) in period $i = 1, 2$. The wage rate is simply the marginal productivity of labor and the land rent is the residual of output over wage costs.

In this model the government provides the public goods in each period and finances them by a lump-sum tax $(T)$ that is imposed on the dynasty as a whole. Notice that in our model a head tax is not a lump-sum tax, since the number of children is endogenous. This is the reason for imposing a fixed tax $T$ on the whole dynasty rather than a head tax on each of its members. The government budget constraint is written as

(7.5)                                  $P^1 + P^2 = T.$

The government is thus restricted to a balanced budget over the whole horizon rather than at each period.[4]

We consider here any arbitrary pair $(P^1, P^2)$ of public good provisions; this vector includes the optimal pair under any desired objective. We show below that there is no market failure, despite a seemingly noninternalized benefit that a greater population size has a lower per capita cost of providing the public good. Since we are considering any pair of public good provisions, our result holds whether or not the government optimizes with respect to the provision of public goods.

The parent in period 1 maximizes her utility function subject to her budget constraint. The utility function is similar to the one in Chapter 6, except that it now includes public goods:

(7.6)                                  $u(c^1, c^2, n, P^1, P^2).$

Obviously, $P^1$ and $P^2$ are not choice variables by the parent, so that the utility maximization is carried out with respect to $c^1$, $c^2$, and $n$, subject to the budget constraint:

(7.7)                    $c^1 + nc^2 = w^1 + nw^2 + \Pi^1 + \Pi^2 - T.$

The parent who cares about her children makes plans for their consumption, taking into account their earnings $(nw^2)$ and the land rent $(\Pi^2)$ accruing to them in the second period. She also takes into acount the entire tax bill $(T)$ of the dynasty. The fact that the children as a group receive both labor income and land rent is really the key to our conclusion.

Given the choice of $P^1$, $P^2$, and $T$ by the government within the budget constraint (7.5), a competitive equilibrium is a 7-tuple $(\tilde{w}^1, \tilde{w}^2, \tilde{\Pi}^1, \tilde{\Pi}^2, \tilde{c}^1, \tilde{c}^2,$

$\tilde{n}$) of wage rates, land rents, parent and child consumptions, and number of children such that: (i) $(\bar{c}^1, \bar{c}^2, \bar{n})$ maximizes (7.6), subject to (7.7), i.e., the parent maximizes her utility subject to her budget constraint; and (ii) the wage rates and land rents are compatible with firm profit maximization, i.e., $\tilde{w}^1, \tilde{w}^2, \tilde{\Pi}^1$, and $\tilde{\Pi}^2$, are given by (7.4).

The main result is summarized in the following proposition:

*Proposition.* A competitive equilibrium is efficient from the current generation point of view: any other feasible allocation (i.e., one that satisfies the resource constraint (7.3)) cannot yield a higher utility to any parent, who already takes into account the welfare of her offspring.

*Proof.* Let $(\tilde{w}^1, \tilde{w}^2, \tilde{\Pi}^1, \tilde{\Pi}^2, \tilde{c}^1, \tilde{c}^2, \tilde{n})$ be a competitive equilibrium and suppose, contrary to the assertion of the proposition, that there exists another feasible allocation $(\bar{w}^1, \bar{w}^2, \bar{\Pi}^1, \bar{\Pi}^2, \bar{c}^1, \bar{c}^2, \bar{n})$ such that

$$u(\bar{c}^1, \bar{c}^2, \bar{n}, P^1, P^2) > u(\tilde{c}^1, \tilde{c}^2, \tilde{n}, P^1, P^2).$$

It follows that the parent could not have afforded the triplet $(\bar{c}^1, \bar{c}^2, \bar{n})$ when faced with the market prices $\tilde{w}^1, \tilde{w}^2, \tilde{\Pi}^1$, and $\tilde{\Pi}^2$: i.e.,

(7.8) $$\bar{c}^1 + \bar{n}\bar{c}^2 > \tilde{w}^1 + \bar{n}\tilde{w}^2 + \tilde{\Pi}^1 + \tilde{\Pi}^2 - T.$$

Adding the government's budget constraint (7.3) to (7.8) yields:

(7.9) $$\bar{c}^1 + \bar{n}\bar{c}^2 + P^1 + P^2 > \tilde{w}^1 + \bar{n}\tilde{w}^2 + \tilde{\Pi}^1 + \tilde{\Pi}^2.$$

At the wage rate $\tilde{w}^2$, firms, by the definition of a competitive equilibrium, maximize profits by hiring $\tilde{n}$ laborers. Their profit is then $\tilde{\Pi}^2$. This maximized profit must be no lower than the profit obtained when hiring $\bar{n}$ laborers. which is $f(\bar{n}) - \bar{n}\tilde{w}^2$. *Thus:*

(7.10) $$\tilde{\Pi}^2 \geq f(\bar{n}) - \bar{n}\tilde{w}^2.$$

Also, from (7.4):

(7.11) $$\tilde{\Pi}^1 = f(1) - \tilde{w}^1.$$

Substituting (7.10) and (7.11) into (7.9) yields

$$\bar{c}^1 + \bar{n}\bar{c}^2 + P^1 + P^2 > f(1) + f(\bar{n}).$$

in violation of the resource constraint (7.3). Thus the proposition is proved.

We can also provide an intuitive explanation of this result that there is no market failure. A market failure arises whenever there is a difference between private and social valuation of *marginal* costs or benefits. Such a difference in the valuation of marginal changes in the *endogenous* variables $c^1$, $c^2$, and $n$ does not arise here. On the benefit side, both the private and the social objectives are represented by the parent's utility (7.6), since one is concerned only with the parent's welfare (who is concerned about her offspring). On the cost side, the parent's perception of the costs associated with $c^1$, $c^2$, and $n$ is derived from her budget constraint (7.7), which can be rewritten as

$$(7.7')\qquad\qquad c^1 + n(c^2 - w^2) + T = w^1 + \tilde{\Pi}^1 + \tilde{\Pi}^2.$$

The social costs are given by the resource constraint (7.3), which can be rewritten as

$$(7.3')\qquad\qquad c^1 + nc^2 - f(n) + P^1 + P^2 = f(1).$$

It is evident from (7.3') and (7.7') that there is no difference between the private and social marginal cost of $c^1$ and $c^2$ (which are 1 and $n$, respectively, both for the parent and for society). The private marginal cost of $n$ is seen from (7.7') to be $c^2 - w^2$. The social marginal cost of $n$ is seen from (7.3') to be $c^2 - f'(n)$. Recalling that, at equilibrium, $w^2 = f'(n)$ (see (7.4)), it follows that there is no difference between the private and social marginal costs of children.

   There is another way to show why there is no market failure in relation to population size. Although the total cost of providing a public good does not fall as the number of children rises, the *average* does fall, but this effect is fully internalized by the parent. Since the parent cares about her children, she is concerned with the total tax bill that the dynasty will have to pay. Having more children may indeed reduce the parent's share in the dynasty tax bill, but since she cares about her children she is concerned not only about her share but also about the total dynasty tax. The only way by which the parent can benefit from a large population is if the number of dynasties increases. But this number is not endogenous. Starting at period 1, there is a fixed number of parents (dynasties), determined in the past.

   Note however, that if marriages between dynasties are allowed, a market failure could arise. In this case children who marry children from another dynasty reduce the average tax burden on each original member of the other dynasty and vice versa. Thus, there is an external economy to the number of children that is not internalized by the heads of dynasties. A similar kind of externality associated with marriage also applies to intergenerational transfers: the transfer that parents make to their child also benefits the parents of the spouse of the child. This particular issue is dealt with in the next chapter, but the same framework can be easily applied here to study the external economy due to interdynasty marriage that arises in the presence of public goods.

## 2. Efficiency with Infinite Overlapping Generations

A puzzling result regarding market failure is obtained by Samuelson (1958) in his exact comsumption-loan model. He shows that under the conventional assumptions on the economic environment, the fact that "... each and every today is followed by a tomorrow ..." may lead competitive markets to fail in achieving the standard Pareto-efficiency objective (Samuelson, 1958, p. 482). Since the standard sources for market failure (externalities and non-convexities) are absent from Samuelson's model, it is natural to try to identify the causes of this inefficiency.[5]

Samuelson's model treats the size of the population as exogenously determined. In this section we show that if endogenous fertility is introduced to Samuelson's model, the inefficiency does not arise. In the analysis presented below, population is an endogenous variable because fertility is; more importantly, endowments of children are assumed to be bequeathed to them by parents. Under the assumptions of perfect capital markets and perfect foresight, it is shown that every competitive equilibrium is Pareto efficient. Note again that in a model with changing population the definition of Pareto efficiency (see Chapter 2) merits some elaboration: Whose utility, that of the current generation alone or of the current and all future (yet unborn) generations, does one wish to include in the efficiency calculation? In our model, there is a direct utility link between each generation and the one immediately following it (and thus an indirect utility link extending into the infinite future), so that the welfare of all generations as perceived by the current one is taken into account by the efficiency criterion.

While the pathological behavior of competitive markets in the Samuelsonian model must indeed be attributed to the infinity of the economy's time horizon (in the sense that in finite-horizon economies the efficiency of competition is guaranteed even under Samuelson's formulation of exogenous population evolution), the fact that in our model each representative individual has an infinite time horizon (even though she lives only a finite time) is shown to be sufficient to restore the efficiency properties of competitive markets.

### 2.a. A review of Samuelson's Model

We first review briefly the essence of Samuelson's inefficiency result as presented in Gale (1973).

Consider an overlapping generations model in which each individual lives for two periods. Each individual is endowed with a vector, $e = (e_0, e_1)$, where $e_i \geq 0$ represents the endowment of the individual in the $i$th period of her life ($i = 0, 1$). Each individual as a parent brings $n$ children into the world at the end of the first period of her life (the beginning of the second period of her life); Samuelson's model assumes that $n$ is an exogenous variable. In addition, all people of all generations are assumed to be identical in endowments and preferences, goods do not keep, and production is ruled out.

Let $c(s) = (c_0(s), c_1(s))$ be the consumption vector of an individual born at the beginning of period $s$, where $c_i(s)$ is the consumption of an individual of age $i$ born at the beginning of period $s$. Following the assumption that nothing is thrown away, the economy's resource constraint in period $s$ is given by

$$(7.12) \qquad n(e_0 - c_0(s)) + (e_1 - c_1(s - 1)) = 0,$$

since there are $n$ young individuals for each old one.

We assume that the representative person has a preference ordering on her lifetime consumption vector that can be represented by a continuous, monotone increasing and quasiconcave utility function. The utility function of an individual born in period $s$ is denoted by $u(c_0(s), c_1(s))$. Recall that both the quantity and quality of children are assumed exogenous, so that they are excluded from the utility function. As usual, a perfect foresight competitive equilibrium is an infinite sequence of interest factors, $\{R(s)\}_{s=0}^{\infty}$, and a feasible consumption program such that each individual maximizes utility subject to the budget constraint defined parametrically by the interest factors:

$$(7.13) \qquad R(s)[e_0 - c_0(s)] + e_1 - c_1(s) = 0.$$

Restricting our attention in this subsection to steady-state equilibrium (namely $c_0(s) = c_0$, $c_1(s) = c_1$ and $R(s) = R$ for all $s$), it is easy to see that these must satisfy

$$(7.14) \qquad (R - n)(e_0 - c_0) = 0.$$

Thus, steady-state equilibria are of two types: those for which $R = n$, the golden-rule program, and those for which $e_0 = c_0$, i.e., autarkic (no-trade) equilibria.

Denoting by $\bar{c}$ the golden-rule program, Figure 7.1 summarizes the possibilities for steady-state equilibrium. The figure demonstrates the possibility of steady-state competitive inefficiency; it obtains at the nontrade equilibrium represented by point $\tilde{e} = (\tilde{e}_0, \tilde{e}_1) = (\tilde{c}_0, \tilde{c}_1)$ and $\tilde{R} < n$. At this point the consumer's marginal rate of substitution is equal to $\tilde{R}$, which is, by (7.13), the private price ratio between future and present consumption faced by the consumer. The inefficiency is illustrated by the fact that in this situation the economy could instantaneously move to $\bar{c}$, making both the existing present generation and all future generations better off: The existing generation consumes $\bar{c}_1$ instead of $\tilde{c}_1$, and future generations move from $\tilde{e}$ to $\bar{c}$, which lies on a higher indifference curve.

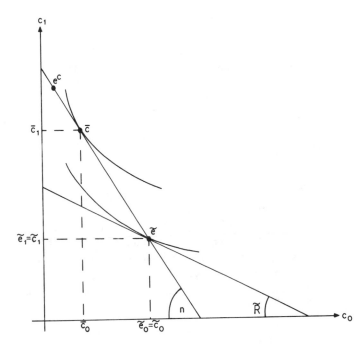

**Figure 7.1.** Possible Steady-State Equilibria.

## 2.b. *Competitive Efficiency when Parents Care about their Children*

A fundamental objection to the Samuelsonian model is that while new generations are continually being produced by the older ones, there is nothing in the model that rationalizes this reproductive behavior. This difficulty is again resolved by our approach, which implies that parents have preferences for children. In the Samuelsonian framework, there is no utility link between any two successive generations. If, on the other hand, there is a link via parents having the utility function of their children as an argument in their own utility function, then, recursively, the utility functions of *all* the (infinitely many) future generations become arguments in each representative individual's utility function. We show below that under this specification of intergenerational preferences perfect foresight competitive equilibria are always efficient.

For each individual born in period $s$ ($s = 0, 1, \ldots$), the utility function is now assumed to be

$$(7.15) \qquad u(c_0(s), c_1(s), n(s), u(c_0(s + 1), c_1(s + 1), n(s + 1), u(\ldots))),$$

where $n(s)$ is the number of children of the representative individual of generation $s$ ($s = j, j + 1, \ldots$). The utility function $u$ is assumed to be monotonically increasing and continuous. The function $u$ should be thought of as a representation of the family's ordinal (Bergson-Samuelson) social welfare function as viewed by the current parent. We assume that each individual is consistent in her planning in the sense of Strotz (1956). Note that consistency with respect to plans of future generations is explicitly embedded in the dynamic programming formulation of the utility function (7.15). Thus, each individual will find it in her interest to carry on the program designed by her ancestors because the latter respect the preferences of their successors.[6] Note also that a measure of the degree of altruism towards future generations (a rate of time preference) is already embedded in the general utility specification.

In order to define an individual's maximization problem in a competitive economy, one must first define the budget set she confronts. On the assumption that there exist perfect capital markets[7] in which each individual of generation $s$ ($s = 0, 1, 2, \dots$) can borrow and lend at the same (parametrically given) interest rates, one can lump together all the individual budget constraints of the members of family $f$ ($f = 1, \dots, F$), where $F$ is the number of families (assumed to be fixed). The present value budget constraint that a family eventually confronts at time $j$ is given by

(7.16)
$$\sum_{i=j}^{\infty} \left[ \left( \prod_{s=j}^{i-1} \frac{n^f(s-1)}{R(s)} \right) (c_1^f(i-1) + n^f(i-1)c_0^f(i)) \right.$$
$$\left. - e_1^f(i-1) - n^f(i-1)e_0^f(i)) \right] - B^f(j) \leq 0$$

where $B^f(j) = \sum_{i=0}^{j-1} (\prod_{s=i}^{j-1} n^f(s-1)R(s))[e_1^f(i-1) + n^f(i-1)e_0^f(i) - c_1^f(i-1) - n^f(i-1)c_0^f(i)]; j = 0, 1, \dots; f = 1, \dots, F;$ and $R(s)$ is the interest factor (one plus the interest rate) prevailing between $s$ and $s+1$.

The meaning of $B^f(j)$ is the value, per individual of age 1 belonging to family $f$, at time $j$ of the cumulative net intergenerational transfers of wealth between period 0 and period $j$, appropriately compounded, assuming that $B^f(0) = 0$.

At time $j$, the economy-wide resource availability constraint is

(7.17)
$$\sum_{f=1}^{F} \left( \prod_{s=0}^{j-1} n^f(s-1) \right) \left[ n^f(j-1)(e_0^f(j) - c_0^f(j)) \right.$$
$$\left. + e_1^f(j-1) - c_1^f(j-1) \right] \geq 0,$$

for every $j = 0, 1, \dots$ Note that $\prod_{s=0}^{j-1} n^f(s-1)$ is the number, at time $j$, of age 1 individuals in family $f$. From (7.16) and (7.17) it is clear that for any $j$ the aggregate cumulative net intergenerational transfers of wealth is nonnegative, namely

$$(7.18) \qquad \sum_{f=1}^{F} \left( \prod_{s=0}^{j-1} n^f(s-1) \right) B^f(j) \geq 0, \qquad j = 0, 1, \ldots .$$

Given $(c_1^f(-1), n^f(-1))$, a perfect foresight competitive equilibrium is defined by nonnegative sequences $\{c_0^f(s), c_1^f(s), n^f(s), R(s)\}_{s=0}^{\infty}$, which satisfy (7.17) such that for each $f$ and $j$, $\{c_0^f(s), c_1^f(s), n^f(s)\}_{s=j}^{\infty}$ maximize (7.15) subject to (7.16).[8] Such an equilibrium is referred to as an infinite-horizon competitive equilibrium.

*Proposition.* An infinite-horizon competitive equilibrium is Pareto efficient.

*Proof.* The proof is standard. Suppose not, and let $\{\tilde{c}_0^{f_0}(s), \tilde{c}_1^{f_0}(s), \tilde{n}^{f_0}(s)\}_{s=j}^{\infty}$ for some $f_0$ and some $j$ be strictly preferred to the competitive sequence $\{c_0^{f_0}(s), c_1^{f_0}(s), n^{f_0}(s)\}_{s=j}^{\infty}$.

By the individual maximization property, it must then be true that

$$(7.19) \qquad \sum_{i=j}^{\infty} \left[ \left( \prod_{s=j}^{i-1} \frac{\tilde{n}^{f_0}(s-1)}{R(s)} \right) (\tilde{c}_1^{f_0}(i-1) + \tilde{n}^{f_0}(i-1)\tilde{c}_0^{f_0}(i) \right.$$

$$\left. - e_1^{f_0}(i-1) - \tilde{n}^{f_0}(i-1)e_0^{f_0}(i)) \right] > \tilde{B}^{f_0}(j).$$

Aggregating (7.19) over the population at time $j$ and using (7.18), a contradiction to (7.17) results. Thus, an infinite-horizon competitive equilibrium must be Pareto efficient.

The no-trade (steady-state) allocation can never be an infinite-horizon competitive equilibrium in the Samuelsonian case, in which the endowment vector $\tilde{e}$ is to the right of the golden-rule allocation in Figure 7.1. As noted by Samuelson (1958) and further elaborated by Gale (1973), the interest rate associated with the no-trade situation in such a case must be lower than the rate of population growth. In our model, however, such an equilibrium relationship between the rate of interest and the rate of population growth can never obtain since it would imply that the budget constraint (7.16) becomes unbounded, which in turn implies infinite excess demands and thus is inconsistent with any competitive equilibrium.

*2.c.   The Nature of Intergenerational Transfers in the Model*

We assumed that $B^f(0) = 0$, i.e., that the "first" individual of age 1 in the economy has no net claims on the present originating in the past. If it is also assumed that all individuals are identical in preferences and endowments, it follows that in equilibrium, $B^f(j) = 0$ for all $f$ and $j$. Note that $B^f(j) > 0$ for some $j$ implies that every family at time $j$ will consume less than the value of its initial endowments. Since goods are desirable and do not keep, the resulting excess supply at time $j$ is inconsistent with equilibrium. Likewise, $B^f(j) < 0$ is impossible since it violates the feasibility condition (there can be no accumulation of goods from the past or decumulation from the future since goods are assumed to be nontransferable across time).

However, in the more general case in which families differ, these conditions will no longer be generally true. While for the economy as a whole the aggregate value in (7.18) is identically equal to zero at all $j$ (the value of aggregate consumption during any time period equals the value of endowments in the same period), it is generally to be expected that some families overconsume in some periods (implying that some other families choose to underconsume in an offsetting way). From (7.16), it is then seen that the existence of overconsuming families until time $j - 1$ implies that in time $j$ the budget constraint includes a negative $B^f(j)$ term.

We wish now to indicate how an institutional setting in which bequests might seemingly be negative is enforceable in a competitive market economy.[9] Bequests from generation $j$ to generation $j + 1$ (intergenerational net transfers of wealth) in this section are effectively always nonnegative in the following sense: If one considers the endowments $e_0$ and $e_1$ (say, productive abilities in each of the periods during which any individual lives) to be inherited (i.e., bequeathed by the previous generation), the possibility that some generations might face a present value of a consumption possibility constraint smaller than the present value of endowments is not to be understood as involving a negative bequest. As long as each generation is able to consume at all (possibly by shifting debt to future generations), it is to be regarded as having obtained a positive bequest from the previous generation.

Property rights in this model are in this sense assigned to parents. Since every individual in the model is a potential parent, this assignment of property rights treats each generation symmetrically. The importance of this condition stems from the fact that if each pair $e_0$ and $e_1$ were assumed to belong to the corresponding generation, then, without outside legislative fiat requiring children to pay their parents' "debts" (i.e., without symmetric inheritance laws that treat debts and gifts in the same way), the above competitive program could not be sustained.

Note that the enforcement of this system of property rights involves more contrivance than the standard one implicitly assumed in finite-horizon intertemporal economies in which each individual is always required to pay her own debts even though this may be contrary to her self-interest (as is the case, for instance, when repayment of debt is due in the individual's last period of life). If the utility links are such that parents' welfare also enter childrens' utility function, then there is an added incentive for children to repay their parents' debts. In any case, the problem of enforcement of negative intergenerational transfers is not a trivial one. In the next chapter, we discuss cases in which we assume that such an enforcement is impossible and therefore consider second-best policy interventions.

## Appendix

We present here an infinite-horizon version of the model presented in Section 1; this model deals with pure public goods and Malthusian fixed land.

### A.1. The Model

**(a) Households.** Consider an overlapping generation model of identical households and an infinite horizon.[10] Each person lives for two periods: in the first period as a child and in the second period as an adult. An adult person of generations $s$ (born at $s - 1$) provides one unit of labor, brings to the world $n_s$ identical children, and consumes together with them a private good, $c_s$, and a pure public good, $P_s$.

As always, it is assumed that parents care about the number and welfare of their children. Since the welfare of these children depends in turn on the number and welfare of their children, and so on, the utility function of an adult person at time 0 can be written as

$$(7.20) \qquad u = u(c_0, n_0, P_0, u(c_1, n_1, P_1, u(\ldots))).$$

We emphasize again that parents determine the number of their children in such a way as to maximize utility. Therefore, a head tax that is usually regarded as a nondistortionary lump-sum tax is no longer so in our model, because a head tax is a tax on the number of children (which is endogenous). For this reason a nondistortionary tax must be imposed on the dynasty as a whole regardless of the number of children born to the dynasty in each time period.

The budget constraint facing the adult at time 0 is

$$(7.21) \qquad c_0 + n_0 b_0 \le w_0 + \Pi_0 - T_0,$$

where $w_0$ is the wage rate, $\Pi_0$ is the rent on the fixed land owned by members of the dynasty, $b_0$ is the amount of bequest that the parent passes on to each one of her $n_0$ children, and $T_0$ is the lump-sum tax paid by the dynasty at time 0.[11] Note again that the total sum of this tax does not depend on the number of children, since otherwise it will become a distortionary tax that creates inefficiencies. More generally, at time $s > 0$, each adult of the dynasty faces the following budget constraint:

$$(7.22) \quad c_s + n_s b_s \leq w_s + \Pi_s/N_{s-1} - T_s/N_{s-1} + Rb_{s-1}, \quad s = 1, 2, \ldots,$$

where $R$ is the interest factor earned on bequests and $N_{s-1} = n_0 n_1 n_2 \ldots n_{s-1}$. We have implicitly assumed that the fixed land is bequeathed in equal shares from one generation to another. Therefore each adult at time $s$ receives a rent of $\Pi_s/N_{s-1}$ because there are $n_{s-1}$ adult members of the dynasty in period $s$. Each adult at time $s$ pays a lump-sum tax of $T_s/N_{s-1}$.

Substituting consecutive budget constraints, one can consolidate them into a single present-value budget constraint for the whole dynasty:

$$(7.23) \quad \sum_{s=0}^{\infty} N_{s-1} D^s c_s + \lim_{s \to \infty} N_s D^s b_s \leq \sum_{s=0}^{\infty} N_{s-1} D^s w_s + \sum_{s=0}^{\infty} D^s \Pi_s$$
$$- \sum_{s=0}^{\infty} D^s T_s,$$

where

$$(7.24) \qquad\qquad N_{s-1} \equiv n_0 n_1 n_2 \ldots n_{s-1}$$

is the number of adults living at time $s$ ($n_{-1}$ is assumed to be equal to 1) and

$$(7.25) \qquad\qquad D^s = R^{-s}$$

is the discount factor from time $s$ to time 0.

Since no one derives a direct utility from bequests ($b_s$ does not enter the utility function of any generation), one can increase $c_s$ without bound (at each $s$) by letting $N_s D^s b_s$ approach $-\infty$. Intuitively, each generation can consume as much as it desires by leaving a sufficiently large and negative bequest to the next generation, which, in turn, can do exactly the same thing and so on. In other words, if $b_s$ can be reduced to $-\infty$ sufficiently fast so that $N_s D^s b_s$ approaches $-\infty$ even though $N_s D^s$ may be tending to zero, then utility can be increased without bound. To avoid this uninteresting possibility, we impose the institutional constraint that $\lim_{s \to \infty} N_s D^s b_s = 0$ and (7.23) becomes[12]

$$(7.23') \quad \sum_{s=0}^{\infty} N_{s-1} D^s c_s \leq \sum_{s=0}^{\infty} N_{s-1} D^s w_s + \sum_{s=0}^{\infty} D^s \Pi_s - \sum_{s=0}^{\infty} D^s T_s.$$

The adult at time 0 then chooses $\{c_s, n_s\}_{s=0,\ldots,\infty}$ so as to maximize the utility function (7.20) subject to the budget constraint (7.23'). Although the adult at period 0 cannot determine $c_s$ and $n_s$ for the future generations, she can plan the sequence $\{c_s, n_s\}_{s=1,\ldots,\infty}$ and, in fact, her offspring will follow this plan by maximizing their own utility. This result occurs because we have assumed that the preferences of an adult in generation $i$ over $\{c_i, n_i\}$ $i = s$, $s + 1, \ldots \infty$ are the same as those of her predecessors. (Her utility is an argument in the utility function of each of her predecessors.) The amount of the public goods $P_0, P_1, \ldots$ are taken by each individual as given.

**(b) Production.** We simplify the production side as much as possible. As in the text, we assume there is a fixed amount of land available in each period. Land is used in each period together with labor to produce an all-purpose good that is used as private or public consumption and also as investment. Since land is fixed, it is suppressed from the production function, which is written as $f(N)$ with $f' > 0$ and $f'' < 0$, i.e., $f$ has positive but (Malthusian) decreasing marginal productivity of labor.

A profit-maximizing firm employs labor and land until, at equilibrium,

(7.26) $$f'(N_{s-1}) = w_s,$$

and

(7.27) $$f(N_{s-1}) - w_s N_{s-1} = \Pi_s.$$

The investment sector is also very simple: A unit of investment made in period $s$ grows (using no other inputs) to be $R$ units in period $s + 1$. In this way the interest factor is fixed and equal to $R$ at equilibrium. Given such investment opportunities, the resource constraint does not require that the sum of private and public consumption in each period may not exceed output in that period, but only that the present value of consumption will not exceed the present value of production:[13]

(7.28) $$\sum_{s=0}^{\infty} N_{s-1} D^s c_s + \sum_{s=0}^{\infty} D^s P_s \le \sum_{s=0}^{\infty} D^s f(N_{s-1}).$$

**(c) Government.** The government provides a sequence of public goods $\{P_s\}_{s=0,\ldots,\infty}$ and finances them by a sequence of lump-sum taxes $\{T_s\}_{s=0,\ldots,\infty}$ subject to its present-value budget constraint:

(7.29) $$\sum_{s=0}^{\infty} D^s P_s = \sum_{s=0}^{\infty} D^s T_s.$$

As in the text, any *arbitrary* sequence $\{P_s\}_{s=0,\ldots,\infty}$ of public good provisions can be considered, including the optimal sequence under any desired objective. There will be no market failure, despite a seemingly noninternalized benefit: a greater population size has a lower per capita cost of providing the public good. Our result holds whether or not the government optimizes with respect to the provision of public goods.

**(d) Competitive Equilibrium.** Given the choice of $\{P_s\}_{s=0,\dots,\infty}$ and $\{T_s\}_{s=0,\dots,\infty}$ by the government, competitive equilibrium is an infinite sequence $[w_s, \Pi_s, c_s, n_s\}_{s=0,\dots,\infty}$ of wage rates, land rents, consumptions, and number of children, such that: (i) the sequence $\{c_s, n_s\}_{s=0,\dots,\infty}$ is optimal for the adult at time 0, i.e., it maximizes her utility function (7.20) subject to her budget constraint (7.23'); (ii) the sequence $\{w_s, \Pi_s\}_{s=0,\dots,\infty}$ is given by (7.26) and (7.27), i.e., the wage rates and the land rents are compatible with firms' profit maximization at each $s$; (iii) the sequence $[c_s, n_s, P_s\}_{s=0,\dots,\infty}$ satisfies the resource constraint (7.28).

## A.2.  Efficiency

As in the text, we can establish the efficiency of the competitive equilibrium.

*Proposition.*  A competitive equilibrium is efficient from the point of view of adults of the current generation: i.e., any other possible allocation cannot yield a higher utility to a member of this generation who already takes into account the welfare of her offspring.

*Proof.*  Let $[\bar{w}_s, \bar{\Pi}_s, \bar{c}_s, \bar{n}_s\}_{s=0,\dots,\infty}$ be a competitive equilibrium and let $\{\tilde{c}_s, \tilde{n}_s\}_{s=0,\dots,\infty}$ be a feasible allocation that yields a higher utility level to the members of the current generation. By utility maximization, it follows that $\{\tilde{c}_s, \tilde{n}_s\}_{s=0,\dots,\infty}$ must violate the budget constraint (7.23'), i.e.,

$$(7.30) \qquad \sum_{s=0}^{\infty} \tilde{N}_{s-1}D^s\tilde{c}_s > \sum_{s=0}^{\infty} \tilde{N}_{s-1}D^s\bar{w}_s + \sum_{s=0}^{\infty} D^s\bar{\Pi}^s - \sum_{s=0}^{\infty} D^sT_s,$$

where

$$\tilde{N}_{s-1} = \tilde{n}_0\tilde{n}_1\tilde{n}_2\dots\tilde{n}_{s-1}.$$

By profit maximization, it follows that

$$(7.31) \qquad \bar{\Pi}_s = f(\bar{N}_{s-1}) - \bar{N}_{s-1}\bar{w}_s \ge f(\tilde{N}_{s-1}) - \tilde{N}_{s-1}\bar{w}_s,$$

where

$$\bar{N}_{s-1} = \bar{n}_0\bar{n}_1\bar{n}_2\dots\bar{n}_{s-1}.$$

Combining (7.30) and (7.31) with the government's budget constraint (7.29) yields

$$\sum_{s=0}^{\infty} \tilde{N}_{s-1}D^s\tilde{c}_s > \sum_{s=0}^{\infty} D^sf(\tilde{N}_{s-1}) - \sum_{s=0}^{\infty} D^sP_s,$$

in violation of the resource constraint (7.28). Therefore, the proposition is proved.

## Notes

1. Spengler (1966) provides a thorough review of this Malthusian kind of externality. See also Nerlove *et al.* (1982) and Willis (1981).
2. A similar reduction in cost is also present in the theory of clubs (e.g., Berglas, 1976). As the public good is usually congestion-prone in that theory, the cost-reduction benefit has to be weighed against the disutility from congestion.
3. In a closed economy, $b$ must be nonnegative. In this chapter we simply assume that this constraint is not binding. In the next chapter we study some of the implications of a similar restriction.
4. In fact, it does not matter whether the government is restricted to a balanced budget at each period or only over the whole horizon, because the parent cares for her children. As long as her bequest is strictly positive, she can always use the bequest to undo any intergenerational distribution of taxes by the government.
5. See Gale (1973), Shell (1971), Starrett (1973), Thompson (1967) and Pazner and Razin (1980); particularly noteworthy for this discussion is Thompson's (1967) analysis of the source of inefficiency in Samuelson's model.
6. If parents do not include in their utility function the utility functions of their offspring as such, but rather impose their own tastes on their children (telling the children what they should like or dislike), there is a problem of time inconsistency; the children may not necessarily follow the path designed for them by their parents (see Dasgupta, 1984).
7. On the nature of property rights in these markets, see below.
8. Note that our definition of equilibrium assumes a maximization of (7.15) subject to (7.16) by individuals of age 0 at each time $j$. In this maximization, $c_1^i(j-1)$, $n^i(j-1)$ is taken as given at the level predetermined by the age 0 individuals at time $j-1$.
9. Contrast this explanation to Barro (1974), who imposed a condition equivalent to $B^i(j) \geq 0$.
10. It is straightforward to extend the analysis to the many-type consumer case.
11. The RHS of (7.21) should also include the inheritance $(b_{-1})$ that the adult of time 0 received from her parent. Since $b_{-1}$ is predetermined and does not play any role in this analysis, we set it equal to zero.
12. Strictly speaking, for (7.23) or (7.23') to be generally valid a restriction, if any, on the nonnegativity of bequests has to be nonbinding.
13. This procedure is justified only under the assumption that the investments required to equalize the two sides of (7.28) at each $s$ are nonnegative.

## References

Barro, Robert J. (1974), "Are Government Bonds Net Wealth?" *Journal of Political Economy*, **82**, 1095-1117.

Berglas, E. (1976), "On the Theory of Clubs." *American Economic Review*, **66**(2), 116-121.

Dasgupta, P. (1985), "The Ethical Foundations of Population Policies." In D. Gale Johnson and R. Lee (eds.), *Population and Economic Development*, Washington: National Academy of Sciences.

Edgeworth, F. Y. (1925), *Papers Related to Political Economy*, Vol. 3. London: Macmillan and Company.

Gale, D. (1973), "Pure Exchange Equilibrium of Dynamic Economic Models." *Journal of Economic Theory*, **6**, 12-36.

Nerlove, M., A. Razin and E. Sadka (1982), "Child Allowances, Optimal Population Policy and Intergenerational Justice," Working Paper No. 9-82. Foerder Institute for Economic Research, Tel-Aviv University. Tel-Aviv, Israel.

Pazner, E. A. and A. Razin (1980), "Competitive Efficiency in an Overlapping-Generation Model with Endogenous Population." *Journal of Public Economics*, **13**, 249-258.

Samuelson, P. A. (1958), "An Exact Consumption Loan Model of Interest with or without the Social Contrivance of Money." *Journal of Political Economy*, **66**, 467-82.

Shell, K. (1971), "Notes on the Economics of Infinity." *Journal of Political Economy*, **79**, 1002-11

Spengler, J. J., (March 1966), "The Economist and the Population Question." *American Economic Review*, **56**, No. 1, 1-24.

Starrett, D. A. (1973), "Inefficiency and the Demand for 'Money' in a Sequence Economy." *Review of Economic Studies*, **40**, 437-48.

Strotz, R. H. (1956), "Myopia and Inconsistency in Dynamic Utility Maximization." *Review of Economic Studies*, **23**, 165-80.

Thompson, E. A. (1967), "Intertemporal Utility Functions and the Long-Run Consumption Function." *Econometrica*, **35**, 356-62.

Willis, R. J. (1981), "On the Social and Private Benefits of Population Growth," Mimeo. New York: SUNY at Stony Brook.

CHAPTER **8**

# Real Market Failures

In this chapter we identify two real sources of market failure in relation to intergenerational transfers. These market failures are unique to our model, in which parents care about their children, since in the absence of such care parents will never transfer (bequeath) anything to their children in a world of perfect foresight and lack of any uncertainty about the time of death.

First, consideration of bequests and of marriage suggests a potential source of market failures: If bequests benefit both partners in a marrriage (as a public good within marriage), parents may fail to include benefits to other children's parents in deciding on the amount of bequests to make to each of their own children. Thus, bequests generate an external economy. Second, when children have different abilities, investments in their human capital are not equally productive. If parents cannot enforce transfers among their children, an egalitarian attitude toward children may lead to inefficient investment in human and nonhuman capital. For example, parents may invest too much in the human capital of low-ability children, so that they will be equal (in a utility sense) to their more able siblings. These cases result in laissez-faire inefficiencies. The nature of these inefficiencies is identified in this chapter and remedies are offered.

## 1.  Bequest as a Public Good within Marriage

In our disccussion so far, the only way in which a bequest functions is to increase children's endowments at the expense of their own parents. We now introduce marriage and, therefore, the possibility that the consumption of a couple can also be increased by bequests from one spouse's parents. Because each family derives utility from the bequests of other families through marriages, Pareto efficiency can only be attained if the parents are free to bargain with one another about what each child's family will leave to its children. Such bargaining was common in biblical times (and is still practiced in some less-developed countries), when parents negotiated *neduniahs* (doweries) and *mohars* (bride prices) with one another and when parents had certain property rights in their children. In modern societies, when much of parents' bequests is in the form of human capital (which belongs exclusively to the child), those kinds of property rights are difficult or impossible to enforce and marriages are not "arranged" in this manner by parents. We show that if children are free to choose and marry for "love," that is, on the basis of considerations unrelated to bequests, and if bequests are determined prior to their choices, the level of bequests will be less than a symmetric Pareto-efficient allocation would require. We also show that under a suitable separability assumption, the number of children in each family is larger than it would be in a symmetric Pareto-efficient allocation.

### 1.a.  Formulation and the Competitive Allocation

In order to show how bequests may lead to market failure when fertility is endogenous, we formulate a simple model in which there are two families in the current generation and only two generations (periods). The utility of the parents depends on their own consumption, the number of children they have, and each child's welfare (enjoyment of bequest) in the second period:

$c_i$ = the consumption of the $i$th family in the first period,
$n_i$ = the number of children of the $i$th family,
$b_i$ = the per-child bequest of the $i$th family,
$K_i$ = the resources available to the $i$th family for consumption and
          bequest, $i = 1, 2$.

The total bequest of two children who marry one another will be the sum of the bequests to each child, i.e., $b_1 + b_2$. We assume that this sum is also the consumption of the second generation. If each family's utility function, $u$, is identical and if each family is endowed with the same amount of a resource, $K$, each will behave in an identical manner, so that the number of children available to marry each other will be identical (with no unmarried people and no incest).

The $i$th family chooses $c_i$, $n_i$, and $b_i$ so as to maximize

(8.1) $$u(c_i, n_i, b_1 + b_2),$$

subject to the resource constraint

(8.2) $$K = c_i + b_i n_i,$$

where $b_j, j \neq i$, is taken as a parameter by the $i$th family (called a parametric externality). A competitive (Nash) solution is the 6-tuple $(\bar{c}_1, \bar{n}_1, \bar{b}_1, \bar{c}_2, \bar{n}_2, \bar{b}_2)$ such that $(\bar{c}_i, \bar{n}_i, \bar{b}_i)$ solves the maximization problem (8.1)–(8.2) defined above, $i = 1, 2$. Because of the assumed symmetry,

$$\bar{c}_1 = \bar{c}_2 \equiv \bar{c}, \quad \bar{b}_1 = \bar{b}_2, \equiv \bar{b}, \quad \text{and} \quad \bar{n}_1 = \bar{n}_2 \equiv \bar{n}.$$

The competitive allocation is characterized by the following first-order conditions (assuming an interior solution):

(8.3) $$\frac{u_2(\bar{c}, \bar{n}, 2\bar{b})}{u_1(\bar{c}, \bar{n}, 2\bar{b})} = \bar{b},$$

and

(8.4) $$\frac{u_3(\bar{c}, \bar{n}, 2\bar{b})}{u_1(\bar{c}, \bar{n}, 2\bar{b})} = \bar{n}.$$

These conditions state the familiar equalities between *private* marginal benefits and costs.

### 1.b. Pareto Efficiency

There are many possible Pareto-efficient allocations in this model. We restrict our attention to a symmetric Pareto-efficient allocation that treats the two families equally in order to be able to compare meaningfully the Pareto-efficient allocation to the competitive allocation, which is symmetric.

A symmetric Pareto-efficient allocation $(c^*, n^*, b^*)$ is obtained by a choice of $(c, n, b)$ so as to maximize

(8.5) $$u(c, n, b + b)$$

subject to the *aggregate* resource constraint of the two families:

(8.6) $$K + K = c + bn + c + bn.$$

Thus, this Pareto-efficient allocation yields the highest equal utility to the two families, given their joint resources.

The symmetric Pareto-efficient allocation is characterized by the following first-order conditions (again assuming an interior solution):

$$(8.7) \qquad \frac{u_2(c^*, n^*, 2b^*)}{u_1(c^*, n^*, 2b^*)} = b^*,$$

and

$$(8.8) \qquad \frac{2u_3(c^*, n^*, 2b^*)}{u_1(c^*, n^*, 2b^*)} = n^*.$$

These conditions state the familiar equalities between the *social* marginal benefits and costs.

Obviously, conditions (8.3)–(8.4), which describe the competitive allocation, and conditions (8.7)–(8.8), which describe the symmetric Pareto-efficient allocation, are different. Thus, the competitive allocation is not Pareto efficient. Comparing the right-hand sides of (8.4) and (8.8), one can see the reason for the market failure: the *social* marginal rate of substitution of $c$ for $b$ is twice the *private* marginal rate of substitution of $c$ for $b$. This difference exists because parents are willing to give up their own consumption ($c$) to secure an additional unit of consumption ($b$) only for their own children; they do not take into account the utility they generate for the parents-in-law of their children's increased consumption.

Observe that if, in the competitive case, marriages are "arranged" in such a way as to be a symmetric solution to a cooperative bargaining game (non-Nash), there will be no difference between the competitive and symmetric Pareto-efficient solutions.

## 1.c. Bequests in the Two Cases

Since in the competitive solution each family ignores its contribution to the welfare of another family, through its bequests to its children who are married to the children of the other family, one would expect that too little is bequeathed in the competitive solution in comparison with the symmetric optimum, i.e., that $\bar{b} \leq b^*$. This is indeed the case.[1] To prove the result formally, suppose on the contrary that $\bar{b} > b^*$. Then

$$(8.9) \qquad u(c^*, n^*, b^* + b^*) - u(c^*, n^*, b^* + \bar{b}) < 0,$$

because $u$ is strictly increasing in $b$. Notice that, by definition, the competitive allocation $(\bar{c}, \bar{n}, \bar{b})$ maximizes $u(c, n, b + \bar{b})$ subject to the budget constraint $K = c + bn$. Since the Pareto-efficient allocation $(c^*, n^*, b^*)$ satisfies this same budget constraint (compare (8.2) and (8.6)), it follows that

$$(8.10) \qquad u(c^*, n^*, b^* + \bar{b}) \leq u(\bar{c}, \bar{n}, \bar{b} + \bar{b}).$$

Combining (8.9) and (8.10),

$$u(c^*, n^*, b^* + b^*) < u(\bar{c}, \bar{n}, \bar{b} + \bar{b}),$$

contradicting the Pareto efficiency of $(c^*, n^*, b^*)$. Thus, it is proved that $\bar{b} \le b^*$.

### 1.d. Number of Children in the Two Cases

Let us now compare the number of children in the two solutions. As we have already noted in Chapter 5, the bequest $b$ is the "price" of children in the budget constraint, (8.2) or (8.6) (see also Becker and Lewis, 1973). That $b$ is a price has three implications. First, since $b$ is smaller in the competitive solution, children are essentially "cheaper." Second, there is a smaller real income (welfare) in the competitive solution because of the externality; thus, if children are a normal good, the income effect tends to counteract the price effect. Third, since, in general, the level of bequests affects the marginal rate of substitution between children $(n)$ and family consumption $(c)$, the projection of the indifference map in the $c - n$ plane shifts. Therefore, it is impossible to draw any general conclusions about the relationship between $\bar{n}$ and $n^*$.

When there is weak separability between $(c, n)$ and $b$, there is no shift in the indifference map for consumption and children.[2] In this special case, barring the possibility of a Giffen good, the price effect dominates, and it can be shown that the number of children in the competitive case is larger than in the Pareto-efficient one $(\bar{n} > n^*)$. To prove the result, note that weak separability between $(c, n)$ and $b$ means that the utility function $u(\cdot)$ can be written as

$$u(c_i, n_i, b_1 + b_2) = U(\phi(c_i, n_i), b_1 + b_2).$$

Therefore, $(c^*, n^*)$ must be a solution to the following program:

(8.11)          $$\max_{c,n} \phi(c, n), \quad \text{subject to} \quad K = c + nb^*.$$

Similarly, $(\bar{c}, \bar{n})$ must be a solution to the following program:

(8.12)          $$\max_{c,n} \phi(c, n), \quad \text{subject to} \quad K = c + n\bar{b}.$$

Clearly, (8.11) and (8.12) are standard consumer optimization problems, where $b^*$ and $\bar{b}$, respectively, are the prices of $n$ and where $\phi$ is the "utility" function. The difference between the price of $n$ in the two problems is the only difference between them. Now, if the utility function, $\phi$, does not give rise to Giffen goods, it follows that $n^* < \bar{n}$ because the price of $n$ in (8.11) is higher than the price of $n$ in (8.12).

Without the assumption of weak separability, it is easy to find examples of plausible utility functions for which the number of children in the Pareto-efficient allocation is larger than in the competitive allocation. For example, if utility is of the form

$$U(c_i, \min(n_i, b_1 + b_2)),$$

then $\bar{n}$ must be less than $n^*$, because $\bar{b} < b^*$, and there is a fixed proportion between bequests and number of children.[3]

## 1.e.   A Corrective Policy

We have identified a source of market failure in parents' bequests to their children. If parents do not take into account the effect of their bequests on the welfare of the families to whom they are potentially related by the marriage of their children, they will bequeath too little. In this case bequests should be subsidized on efficiency grounds rather than taxed, which is the standard Pigouvian remedy to an external economy. In the standard economic models of externalities (see Chapter 3), this kind of a Pigouvian subsidy is all that is needed. Only the good that generates an external economy should be subsidized, and only the good that generates an external diseconomy should be taxed. In our case, the bequest generates an external economy. But in this case, it is not sufficient simply to grant an appropriate subsidy to the bequest because the bequest $b$ is also the "price" of $n$. Thus, subsidizing $b$ distorts (i.e., reduces) the price of $n$. This distortion must be removed by an appropriate simultaneous tax on children.

To find the optimal corrective policy in this case, denote by $\alpha$ the subsidy rate to bequests and by $\beta$ the subsidy (child allowance) to children, which could be negative. The parental budget constraint becomes

(8.2′)                      $$K = c_i + b_i(1 - \alpha)n_i - \beta n_i - T,$$

where $T$ is the lump-sum tax that may be needed in order to balance the government's budget. Maximizing the utility function (8.1) with respect to this budget constraint yields the following first-order conditions:

(8.13)                                    $$\frac{u_2}{u_1} = b(1 - \alpha) - \beta,$$

and

(8.14)                                    $$\frac{u_3}{u_1} = (1 - \alpha)n.$$

The optimal (Pigouvian) $\alpha$ and $\beta$ (denoted by $\alpha^*$ and $\beta^*$) can be found by comparing (8.13)–(8.14) with the first-order conditions (8.7)–(8.8), which characterize the symmetric Pareto-efficient allocation. First, comparing (8.8) with (8.14), one can see that $\alpha^*$ must satisfy

$$(1 - \alpha^*)n^* = n^*/2,$$

so that

(8.15)                                    $\alpha^* = 1/2.$

Next, comparing (8.7) with (8.13), one can see that $\beta^*$ must satisfy

$$b^*(1 - \alpha^*) - \beta^* = b^*.$$

Substituting (8.15) into this equality, one sees that:

(8.16)                                $\beta^* = -\tfrac{1}{2}b^* < 0.$

Thus, the corrective policy must have two ingredients. First, there should be a 50 percent subsidy to bequests because the *social* marginal rate of substitution of $c$ for $b$ is always twice the *private* marginal rate of that substitution. Second, because the price of $n$ is distorted downward by $b^*/2$ when bequests are subsidized at a 50 percent rate, there should be a tax of $b^*/2$ per child.

Finally, note that the externality identified here applies not only to bequests in the form of physical capital but also, especially, to bequests in the form of investments in the human capital of children. It is the latter form that effectively prevent establishment of a system of property rights of parents in children that would eliminate the externality.


## 2.  Investment in Human and Physical Capital and Transfers among Siblings

In this section we analyze the consequences for social welfare of the fact that parents cannot control the actions of their children after a certain time. In particular, we explore the implications for efficient allocation of parents' inability to enforce transfers among siblings.

Parents can transfer resources to their children in two major ways: direct transfers of consumption (bequests) or indirect transfers of investment in human capital of their children, which increase the future consumption-possibility sets of the children. The most efficient method of transfer may depend on the specific characteristics of a particular child so that a parent may wish to use different methods for different children. Furthermore, in some cases it may be more efficient to make transfers only to some of the children and force them to make transfers later to the siblings who did not receive transfers from the parent. But this possibly most efficient method of transfers to children depends on a parent's ability to enforce the required transfers among them. This requirement poses a difficulty that cannot be eliminated, not even, for instance, by appeal to Becker's "rotten-kid" theorem or by appeal to vaguely defined social norms (see Becker, 1974, 1976; Hirschleifer, 1977). Becker and Tomes (1976) note the difficulty, but suggest in passing that "... social and family 'pressures' can induce... children to conform to the terms of implicit contracts with their parents." Such norms might be effective in some circumstances in some societies but they have certainly not generally been effective even in ancient societies—as the biblical episode of Cain and Abel attests—let alone in modern societies.

To see that equal transfers to siblings are not efficient even for parents who believe in equity among children, consider the case of children who differ in their abilities. In this case it might be most efficient to invest only in the human capital of the able children if parents could guarantee that the able children would later on transfer part of the return to this investment to their less able siblings. However, if transfers among siblings cannot be enforced by the parents, they may not be able to take advantage of high rates of return to investment in the human capital of their more able children. In this case, transfers in the form of investment in human capital from parents to children will be too low relative to bequests in the form of bequests. Moreover, the investment in human capital will be inefficiently allocated among the children to the extent that the rates of return are not the same for all children.

If children's ability could be identified by the government, a system of taxes and transfers based on ability could be devised in order to achieve an efficient allocation of resources. However, if identification of more able and less able children is impossible or prohibitively costly except for the parents themselves, a first-best solution to the problem of optimal investment in human capital and bequests cannot be achieved. Therefore, we consider various second-best corrective policies, and we show that a linear tax on earned income and a subsidy to inheritance are welfare improving. Such policies make parents better off because they redistribute income from able to less able siblings and allow parents to allocate more efficiently their investments in their children's human and physical capital. Other policies, such as public investment in human capital or a tax or subsidy for education, reduce welfare.

## 2.a.  Formulation of the Model

This model assumes that there are only two periods, two generations, and a single all-purpose composite good. (An infinite-horizon, steady-state version of this model is presented in the appendix to this chapter.) The first generation consists of identical individuals (parents) who live for one period.

But the second generation is not homogenous: proportion $p$ of children has high ability (indexed by $A$), and proportion $1 - p$ has low ability (indexed by $B$). Parents invest $e^A$ and $e^B$ units of the composite good in the education (human capital) of each one of the high ability and low ability children, respectively, and bequeath $b^A$ and $b^B$ units of the composite good to each child of high ability and each child of low ability, respectively.

Each pair of parents is endowed with $K$ units of the composite good. Each child supplies one unit of adult labor in the second period. Investing $e^i$ in the education of a child of ability level $i$ augments its labor supply, as measured in efficiency units, to $g_i(e^i)$, $i = A, B$. It then earns $wg_i(e^i)$, where $w$ is the wage rate per efficiency unit. The difference between the two types of ability is reflected in the functions $g_A$ and $g_B$. It is assumed that $g_A(e) > g_B(e)$ for all $e$, so that the able child is more productive than the less able. Furthermore, the marginal investment in the able child is also assumed to be more productive: $g'_A(e) > g'_B(e)$ for all $e$. We also assume that there are diminishing returns to investing in each child, i.e., $g''_i < 0$, $i = A, B$.

When parents bequeath $b$ units of the composite good, we assume the bequest is invested (in physical capital) and yields $bR$ units to the child as an adult in the second period, where $R \geq 1$ is the interest factor.[4] For the sake of simplicity, $w$ are $R$ are assumed fixed.

We assume that parents treat their children's welfare symmetrically, irrespective of the child's ability, and plan their bequests to each child and investment in that child's education in such a way that each child will be able to consume the same amount, $c^2$, in the second period.[5] As before, the parents' utility function depends on $c^1$, $c^2$, and $n$:

$$(8.17) \qquad\qquad u(c^1, c^2, n).$$

The parents choose $c^1$, $c^2$, and $n$ so as to maximize (8.17), subject to the following budget constraints:

$$(8.18) \qquad K = c^1 + pn(e^A + b^A) + (1 - p)n(e^B + b^B),$$

$$(8.19) \qquad\qquad c^2 = wg_A(e^A) + Rb^A,$$

$$(8.20) \qquad\qquad c^2 = wg_B(e^B) + Rb^B.$$

Constraint (8.18) is the budget constraint of the parents: consumption plus investment in the human and physical capital of the children cannot exceed the parents' endowment. Constraints (8.19) and (8.20) are the budget constraints facing each one of the more able and less able children, respectively, in the second period.

We assume a closed economy in which the total amount of bequests cannot be negative: i.e.,

$$(8.21) \qquad\qquad\qquad pnb^A + (1-p)nb^B \geq 0.$$

Such a constraint is natural in view of the fact that bequests form the economy's capital stock, and in a closed economy resources cannot be transferred backwards from future to present generations. We further assume that no parents can enforce transfers from their offspring to themselves: formally,

$$(8.22) \qquad\qquad\qquad b^A \geq 0, \qquad b^B \geq 0.$$

Constraint (8.21) will be binding whenever there is higher yield to investment in human capital than in physical capital. In this case, in order to equate the marginal yields on all forms of investment (i.e., $wg'_A(e^A) = wg'_B(e^B) = R$), parents may have to direct all investment to human capital and may even wish to transfer physical resources backwards by borrowing (i.e., by making $pnb^A + (1-p)nb^B$ negative), which we have ruled out. Therefore, relaxing constraint (8.21) will be welfare improving in this case. However, (8.21) is a technological constraint that is imposed on the economy and neither individuals nor government can do anything about it. For this reason, we are not interested in analyzing the case in which it (8.21) is binding and assume henceforth that it is not binding.

The situation is rather different with respect to constraint (8.22), which is essentially institutional. It stems from the inability of parents to enforce transfers among siblings. Note that constraints (8.19) and (8.20) disallow *direct* transfers among siblings: each child must consume exactly what the parents transfer to it in the form of human or physical capital. But (8.19) and (8.20) still leave open the possibility that parents make *indirect* transfers among their children. For example, instead of asking child $A$ to make a direct transfer of one dollar to child $B$, the parents can simply reduce the bequest to $A$ ($b^A$) by one dollar and increase the bequest to $B$ ($b^B$) by one dollar. These changes in the bequests (i.e., the *indirect* transfers among siblings) are possible as long as (8.22) is not binding. But if (8.22) is binding, as is the case, for instance, when $b^A$ is already zero, the parents cannot further reduce $b^A$ and cannot therefore achieve a transfer among their children. Thus, the constraint of no transfer among siblings is effective only when (8.22) is binding.

When constraint (8.22) is not binding, maximization of the utility function (8.17) subject to the budget constraints (8.18)–(8.20) implies that $wg'_A(e^A) = R = wg'_B(e^B)$. In this case both the *total* investment in the human and physical capital of each child (namely, $e^i + b^i$) and its *division* between human capital

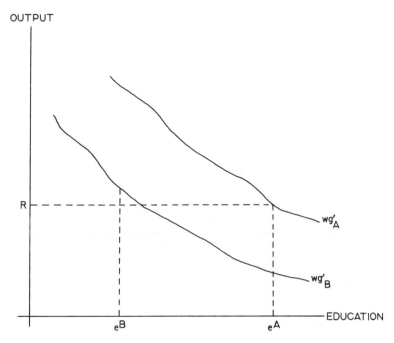

**Figure 8.1.** Return on Investment of Human and Physical Capital in Children of Different Abilities.

$(e^i)$ and physical capital $(b^i)$ are optimally determined. This outcome is achieved by parents' investing in the child's human capital up to the point at which the marginal yield is equal to the interest factor (i.e., $wg_i'(e^i) = R$) and then the $b$'s are adjusted in order to maintain the equality $wg_A(e^A) + b^A = wg_B(e^B) + b^B$ (which is essentially required by (8.19) and (8.20)) and to achieve the total desired level of transfer $(e^i + b^i)$ to each child. This case might be fairly common, but our main purpose is to analyze the case in which constraint (8.22) is binding. In that latter case, the first-order condition $wg_i'(e^i) = R$ must be replaced by $wg_i'(e^i) \geq R$. As we show below, there is an aggregate missallocation between investment in human capital and in physical capital: in particular, parents are forced to invest too little in the human capital of their more able children.

We henceforth assume that (8.22) is binding. But since (8.21) is not binding, both inequalities of (8.22) cannot be binding. Given our assumption about the relationship between $g_A$ and $g_B$, we show that it is the second that is not binding. Suppose to the contrary that $b^B = 0$. Hence, $wg_B'(e_B) \geq R$. Since the first inequality is not binding in this case, it follows that $wg_A'(e^A) = R$. Since $g_A' \geq g_B'$ and both are diminishing (see Figure 8.1), it follows that $e^B < e^A$ and

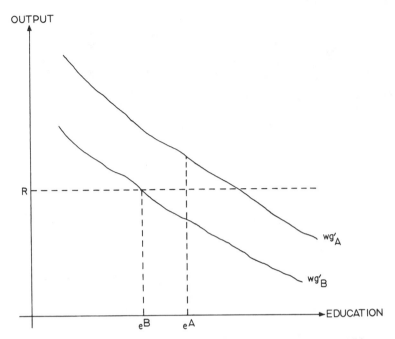

**Figure 8.2.** Returns to Human Capital for More Able and Less Able Children.

hence that $g_B(e^B) < g_A(e^A)$. But since $wg_A(e^A) + b^A R = wg_B(e^B)$, it follows that $b^A < 0$, which is a contradiction. Therefore $b^A = 0$ and $b^B > 0$.

This result means that the rate of return on investment in the human capital of more able children is higher than that on physical capital, i.e., parents would like to borrow from their able children (that is, leave them negative bequests) in order to invest more in their human capital, given the amount of resources they are transferring, but cannot (see Figure 8.2). If transfers among siblings were possible, constraint (8.22) would be effectively eliminated, thus permitting parents to equate rates of return.

In summary, the two ways in which parents might *collectively* enforce transfers among children by government action are only feasible if it is possible to discriminate among children by ability or to enforce obligations imposed upon children by parents. One method is by a system of lump-sum intragenerational transfers based on children's ability. But since individual ability is observable only by parents, such a system for achieving the first-best solution is infeasible. The other method is a system of student loans that would permit parents to equate rates of return on investments in human and physical capital by enabling them to take out loans to finance the education of their more able children and obligating those children to repay the loans in the next period. Such a system of loans achieves a first-best solution, but it rests on the ability of parents to obligate their children to repay loans that the parents took on their behalf. Therefore, in the next section we consider only second-best solutions, i.e., those that alleviate rather than eliminate (8.22).

## 2.b.  A Second-Best Corrective Policy

Among the second-best policy instruments that the government can use we consider three: (i) a linear tax on the earned income of grown-up children in the second period with a marginal rate $t$ and a demogrant $T$; (ii) an inheritance tax at the rate $\tau$, imposed on physical bequests only; (iii) an interest income tax at the rate $\theta$. Some other familiar policies are considered in the next section; they are shown to be either redundant or detrimental. It should be emphasized that taxes (head taxes or others) that discriminate on the basis of ability are not allowed, and this is really the crux of the problem at hand. If such discriminatory taxes were allowed, then we could essentially eliminate constraint (8.22) and achieve a first-best allocation (continuing to assume that (8.21) is not binding).

Given these policy instruments, the constraints (8.18)–(8.20) facing the parents become:

(8.18′)     $$K = c^1 + pn(e^A + b^A) + (1 - p)n(e^B + b^B),$$

(8.19′)     $$c^2 = (1 - t)wg_A(e^A) + T + (1 - \theta')R(1 - \tau)b^A,$$

and

(8.20′)     $$c^2 = (1 - t)wg_B(e^B) + T + (1 - \theta')R(1 - \tau)b^B,$$

where $\theta'$ is the tax rate on the interest factor $(R)$, which is related to the tax rate $(\theta)$ on the interest rate $(R - 1)$ by $(1 - \theta')R = 1 + (1 - \theta)(R - 1)$ or $\theta' = \theta(R - 1)/R$. It is clear from (8.19′) and (8.20′) that either $\theta'$ or $\tau$ is redundant, and therefore we henceforth set $\theta' = \theta = 0$.

The parent maximizes $u(c^1, c^2, n)$, subject to the budget constraints (8.18′)–(8.20′) and the nonnegativity constraint $b^A \geq 0$. The Lagrangian expression is

(8.23)     $$L = u(c^1, c^2, n) + \lambda_1[K - c^1 - pn(e^A + b^A) - (1 - p)n(e^B + b^B)]$$
$$+ \lambda_2[(1 - t)wg_A(e^A) + T + R(1 - \tau)b^A - c^2]$$
$$+ \lambda_3[(1 - t)wg_B(e^B) + T + R(1 - \tau)b^B - c^2]$$
$$+ \lambda_4 b^A,$$

where $\lambda_1 \geq 0$, $\lambda_2 \geq 0$, $\lambda_3 \geq 0$, and $\lambda_4 \geq 0$ are the Lagrange multipliers associated with (8.18′), (8.19′), (8.20′), and (8.22′) respectively. The first-order conditions for $c^1$, $c^2$, $b^A$, $b^B$, $e^A$, $e^B$, and $n$, respectively, are given below:

(8.24) $$u_1 - \lambda_1 = 0,$$

(8.25) $$u_2 - \lambda_2 - \lambda_3 = 0,$$

(8.26) $$-\lambda_1 pn + \lambda_2(1 - \tau)R + \lambda_4 = 0,$$

(8.27) $$-\lambda_1(1 - p)n + \lambda_3(1 - \tau)R = 0,$$

(8.28) $$-\lambda_1 pn + \lambda_2(1 - t)wg'_A = 0,$$

(8.29) $$-\lambda_1(1 - p)n + \lambda_3(1 - t)wg'_B = 0,$$

and

(8.30) $$u_3 - \lambda_1[p(e^A + b^A) + (1 - p)(e^B + b^B)] = 0.$$

The solution to this maximization problem yields $c^1$, $c^2$, $n$, $b^B$, $e^A$, and $e^B$ as functions $\bar{c}^1(\cdot)$, $\bar{c}^2(\cdot)$, $\bar{n}(\cdot)$, $\bar{b}^B(\cdot)$, $\bar{e}^A(\cdot)$, and $\bar{e}^B(\cdot)$, respectively, of the government's instrument vector $(t, T, \tau)$. In addition, of course, $b^A = 0$, by assumption. The indirect utility function is denoted by

$$v(t, T, \tau) \equiv u(\bar{c}^1(t, T, \tau), \bar{c}^2(t, T, \tau), \bar{n}(t, T, \tau)).$$

Let us now turn to the government's budget constraint. In the first period, it has no expenditures or revenues. In the second period, the government collects $ntw[pg_A(e^A) + (1 - p)g_B(e^B)]$ from the marginal tax component of the linear earned income tax; $n(1 - p)\tau b^B R$ from the inheritance tax (recall that $b^A = 0$); and it pays $nT$ in demogrants. Thus, the government must satisfy the following budget constraint:

(8.31) $$T = tw[pg_A(e^A) + (1 - p)g_B(e^B)] + (1 - p)\tau b^B R.$$

Let the government choose its instruments ($t$, $T$, and $\tau$) so as to maximize $v(t, T, \tau)$ subject to its budget constraint (8.31). A first-order characterization of the optimum is straightforward but unfortunately not very informative. We therefore take up the more modest task of looking for welfare-improving directions of tax changes around the no-intervention state, $t = T = \tau = 0$ (the laissez-faire point).

In order to simplify the analysis, we substitute the functions $\bar{c}^1$, $\bar{c}^2$, $\bar{n}$, $\bar{b}^B$, $\bar{e}^A$, and $\bar{e}^B$ in the government's budget constraint (8.31):

(8.32) $$T = tw\{pg_A[\bar{e}^A(t, T, \tau)] + (1 - p)g_B[\bar{e}^B(t, T, \tau)]\}$$
$$+ (1 - p)\tau R\bar{b}^B(t, T, \tau).$$

This equation defines $T$ implicitly as a function $\bar{T}(t, \tau)$ of $t$ and $\tau$. This function means that given the marginal tax rate on earned income ($t$) and the inheritance tax rate ($\tau$), the government has just enough revenues from these taxes to pay a demogrant of $\bar{T}(t, \tau)$.

Total differentiation of (8.32) with respect to $t$ and $\tau$ gives the partial derivatives of $\bar{T}$ with respect to $t$ and $\tau$:

$$(8.33) \qquad \bar{T}_1 = w[pg_A + (1-p)g_B] + twpg'_A(\bar{e}_1^A + \bar{e}_2^A \bar{T}_1)$$
$$+ tw(1-p)g'_B(\bar{e}_1^B + \bar{e}_2^B \bar{T}_1)$$
$$+ (1-p)\tau R(\bar{b}_1^B + \bar{b}_2^B \bar{T}_1),$$

$$(8.34) \qquad \bar{T}_2 = tw[pg'_A(\bar{e}_2^A \bar{T}_2 + \bar{e}_3^A) + (1-p)g'_B(\bar{e}_2^B \bar{T}_2 + \bar{e}_3^B)]$$
$$+ (1-p)R\bar{b}^B + (1-p)\tau R(\bar{b}_2^B \bar{T}_2 + \bar{b}_3^B).$$

Evaluated at $t = \tau = \bar{T}(t, \tau) = 0$, the partial derivatives of $\bar{T}$ are found from (8.33)–(8.34) to be

$$(8.35) \qquad \bar{T}_1 = w[pg_A + (1-p)g_B],$$

and

$$(8.36) \qquad \bar{T}_2 = (1-p)R\bar{b}^B.$$

We can now evaluate the effects of changes in the marginal tax rate on earned income ($t$) and of the inheritance tax rate ($\tau$) and the demogrant ($T$) on welfare. Note, however, that these changes are restricted by the government's budget constraint: Once the changes in $t$ and $\tau$ are chosen, one is no longer free to make any change in $T$ but is restricted to that change in $T$ consistent with the function $\bar{T}(t, \tau)$.

Substituting $\bar{T}(t, \tau)$ for $T$ in the indirect utility function $v(t, T, \tau)$ gives rise to

$$(8.37) \qquad V(t, \tau) \equiv v(t, \bar{T}(t, \tau), \tau).$$

We next evaluate the effect of changes in $t$ and $\tau$ (and the resulting necessary change in $T$, as dictated by the function $\bar{T}$) on parents' welfare ($V$) at the laissez-faire point $t = \tau = \bar{T}(t, \tau) = 0$.

Differentiating (8.37) with respect to $t$ and $\tau$,

$$(8.38) \qquad V_1 = v_1 + v_2 \bar{T}_1,$$

and

$$(8.39) \qquad V_2 = v_2 \bar{T}_2 + v_3.$$

Using the envelope theorem (see the Appendix to Chapter 4), one can calculate $v_1$, $v_2$, and $v_3$ by differentiating partially the Lagrangian expression (8.23):

$$(8.40) \qquad v_1 = -w(\lambda_2 g_A + \lambda_3 g_B),$$

$$(8.41) \qquad v_2 = \lambda_2 + \lambda_3,$$

and

$$(8.42) \qquad\qquad v_3 = -R(\lambda_2 \bar{b}^A + \lambda_3 \bar{b}^B) = -R\lambda_3 \bar{b}^B.$$

Consider first a change in the marginal tax rate $t$ (accompanied by a change in the demogrant $T$) at the laissez-faire point. Substituting (8.35), (8.40), and (8.41) into (8.38), one obtains:

$$(8.43) \qquad V_1 = -w(\lambda_2 g_A + \lambda_3 g_B) + (\lambda_2 + \lambda_3)w[pg_A + (1 - p)g_B]$$
$$= w(g_A - g_B)[\lambda_3 p - \lambda_2(1 - p)].$$

Using (8.27),

$$(8.44) \qquad\qquad (1 - \tau)R = \lambda_1(1 - p)n/\lambda_3.$$

Substituting (8.44) into (8.26) yields

$$-\lambda_1 pn + \lambda_2 \lambda_1(1 - p)n/\lambda_3 + \lambda_4 = 0.$$

Since $\lambda_4 \geq 0$, it follows that

$$(8.45) \qquad\qquad \lambda_3 p - \lambda_2(1 - p) \geq 0.$$

Since $b^B > 0$ while $b^A = 0$, it follows from (8.19′) and (8.20′) that

$$(8.46) \qquad\qquad g_A - g_B > 0.$$

Hence, it follows from (8.43), (8.45), and (8.46) that $V_1 \geq 0$. Thus, some tax on earned income (with a marginal rate $t$ and a demogrant $T$) is welfare improving.

In order to understand the rationale for this result, observe that because the constraint $b^A \geq 0$ is binding, the parents would have liked to increase $e^A$ and lower $b^A$. This is also evident from (8.26) and (8.28), which imply that

$$wg'_A = R + \frac{\lambda_4}{\lambda_2} \geq R,$$

which in turn means that the return to $e^A$ (namely, $wg'_A$) is greater than the return to $b^A$ (namely, $R$). But parents cannot reduce $b^A$ because $b^A$ is already zero. Therefore, the parents cannot further increase $e^A$ without increasing the transfer $npe^A + n(1 - p)(e^B + b^B)$ because, by (8.19′) and (8.20′), $(1 - t)wg_A(e^A)$ must be equated with $(1 - t)wg_B(e^B) + R(1 - \tau)b^B$, so that raising $e^A$ must be accompanied by raising $e^B$ or $b^B$ as well. Since $g_A > g_B$, raising $t$ takes more from the more able than from the less able children, while $T$ is given equally to both kinds of children. Therefore, such an increase in $t$ and $T$ enables parents to increase $e^A$ without additional transfers to their children. In this way, the transfer of wealth from the present to the future is channelled more efficiently and welfare is improved. It should be emphasized that, in this case, income taxation is justified on pure efficiency grounds apart from the common justification on distributional grounds:[6] Knowing that government is redistributing income among siblings enables the parents to channel the transfer of wealth to their offspring more efficiently, thus making the parents, themselves, better off.

We next consider a change in $\tau$ (accompanying by the necessary change in $T$ indicated by the function $\bar{T}$). Substituting (8.36), (8.41), and (8.42) into (8.39), one obtains

$$V_2 = (\lambda_2 + \lambda_3)(1 - p)R\bar{b}^B - \lambda_3 R\bar{b}^B$$

$$= [\lambda_2(1 - p) - \lambda_3 p]R\bar{b}^B \leq 0,$$

by (8.45). Thus, some positive inheritance subsidy (a negative $\tau$), financed by lowering the demogrant component of the tax on earned income, is welfare improving. Here again the inheritance subsidy enables parents to overcome the deficiency in investment in the education of the able children without increasing the total transfer of wealth to their children: the required equality between $(1 - t)wg_A(e^A)$ and $(1 - t)wg_B(e^B) + (1 - \tau)R b^B$ may be preserved when $\tau$ is made negative by increasing $e^A$ and decreasing $b^B$.

## 2.c.  Additional Policies

We have shown here that a linear tax on earned income and a subsidy to inheritance are useful in alleviating the constraint imposed by $b^A \geq 0$, which causes underinvestment in the human capital of able children. We could consider also direct government investment in human capital (free education), but as long as the $e$'s are positive such a policy is redundant. Parents can always undo the effects of such policies by reducing their investments in human capital, dollar for dollar, in response to the government investment. If public investment in human capital is so high so as to make parents wish to have a negative $e^A$ or $e^B$, it is even suboptimal.

Instead of a direct government investment in human capital, one can consider a subsidy to education. A subsidy to education, in the first period, must also be financed by a lump-sum tax in the same period because the government cannot transfer resources from the future to the present. Such a subsidy does not help alleviate constraint (8.22). On the other hand, it creates a distortion by artificially lowering the cost of education to parents; thus, it reduces welfare because parents can achieve the postsubsidy allocation under laissez-faire.[7]

Specifically, if there is a subsidy to education at the rate $s$ and a lump-sum tax, $Y$, in the first period to finance it, the budget constraint of the first period (8.18') changes to

(8.18'')     $K = c^1 + pn[e^A(1 - s) + b^A] + (1 - p)n[e^B(1 - s) + b^B] + Y.$

Now suppose that under these circumstances parents choose $\tilde{c}^1$, $\tilde{n}$, $\tilde{e}^A$, $\tilde{b}^A$, $\tilde{e}^B$, and $\tilde{b}^B$. Since $Y$ is determined by the government so as to just finance the subsidy to education, it follows that

(8.47) $$Y = s\tilde{n}[p\tilde{e}^A + (1 - p)\tilde{e}^B].$$

Equations (8.18″) and (8.47) imply that

(8.48) $$K = \tilde{c}^1 + p\tilde{n}(\tilde{e}^A + \tilde{b}^A) + (1 - p)\tilde{n}(\tilde{e}^B + \tilde{b}^B).$$

Comparing (8.48) with (8.18′) one can see that the postsubsidy choice of parents, $(\tilde{c}^1, \tilde{n}, \tilde{e}^A, \tilde{b}^A, \tilde{e}^B, \tilde{b}^B)$, satisfies the budget constraint that they faced before the subsidy. Thus, they could have chosen the postsubsidy allocation, $(\tilde{c}_1, \tilde{n}, \tilde{e}^A, \tilde{b}^A, \tilde{e}^B, \tilde{b}^B)$, before the subsidy as well, so that the subsidy could not possibly improve their welfare.

## Appendix

In this appendix we present an infinite-horizon, steady-state extension of the model developed in Section 2. Unfortunately, the steady state does not extend the finite-horizon case in a meaningful way, as we show.

In a steady state there is a potential problem of unbounded intergenerational transfers (when $R > n$). Hence, one must drop the assumption that $R$ is fixed; assume instead a neoclassical constant-returns-to-scale production function $F(M, L)$ with diminishing marginal productivities of labor, $L$, and capital, $M$. Assume also that $F$ satisfies the Inada conditions: (i) $F_L$ and $F_M$ are unbounded as $L$ and $M$, respectively, approach zero; and (ii) $F_L$ and $F_M$ approach zero as $L$ and $M$, respectively, increase without bound. Total labor supply in efficiency units is $L = png_A(e^A) + (1 - p)ng_B(e^B)$, and the total stock of capital is $M = pnb^A + (1 - p)nb^B$. In this case, $R - 1 = F_M$ and $w = F_L$.

Consider a steady-state allocation in which each person consumes $c$ units of consumption, irrespective of ability or generation. Denote the wealth of each person by $K$. The constraints (8.18)–(8.20) have to be replaced now by

(8.49) $$K = c + pn(e^A + b^A) + (1 - p)n(e^B + b^B),$$

(8.50) $$K = wg_A(e^A) + Rb^A,$$

and

(8.51) $$K = wg_B(e^B) + Rb^B.$$

Equation (8.49) states that each individual has to allocate her wealth to her consumption and to investments in the human and physical capital of all her children. Equations (8.50) and (8.51) state that children of the two types of ability must have the same wealth $(K)$ transferred to them by their parents.

Assume that the utility $u$ of each person is additively separable, $u = \sum_{t=0}^{\infty} \delta^t U(c^t, n^t)$, with a discount factor $0 < \delta < 1$. In this case a parent's steady-state objective is to maximize $U(c, n)$ subject to (A.1)–(A.3) and the nonnegativity constraint (8.22). Notice that in a steady state $K$ itself is also determined by the parent.

From the individual point of view, $R$ is given. If $R > n$, it follows from (8.49)–(8.51) that $c$ can be increased without bound (keeping $n$ constant) because by (8.50)–(8.51) one can increase $K$ by $R$ units by increasing $b^A$ and $b^B$, each by one unit. The right-hand side of (8.49) in this case is increased only by $pn + (1 - p)n = n$ units, which is smaller than the increase in $K$, thus allowing one to increase $c$. This operation can be repeated indefinitely so that $c$ increases without bound. But then $R$ cannot stay constant; it must fall via the increase in $M$. Similarly, if $R < n$, it pays a parent to reduce $b^A$ and $b^B$ until one of them reaches zero. If both go to zero (and therefore $M$ also goes to zero), $R$ goes to infinity, by the Inada condition, and thus $R$ cannot stay smaller than $n$.

Hence, at equilibrium, either of two conditions exist: (i) the steady-state golden rule, $R = n$, or (ii) $b^A = 0$. In case (i), it is straightforward to see from (8.49)–(8.51) that an individual is indifferent about increasing (or decreasing) both $b^A$ and $b^B$ by the same amount. Hence constraint (8.22) cannot be binding, and there is no role for the government to play. In case (ii), one might repeat the analysis of Section 2. However, since the number of children $(n)$ is itself a choice variable, the steady-state utility is unbounded because in a competitive context, each individual perceives $R$ as constant. Hence, for any given $R$, an individual can reduce $n$ below $R$ and increase consumption and utility without bound.

Note that in a non-steady-state analysis, $K$ of constraint (8.18) is given (that is, it is not a choice variable), which makes utility in Section 2 bounded and the non-steady-state analysis useful. Thus, we see that a steady-state analysis cannot serve as a meaningful extension of the finite-horizon analysis of Section 2.

## Notes

1. As shown in the literature on externalities, this result follows from the assumed symmetry here; see Buchanan and Kafoglis (1963), Diamond and Mirrlees (1973), and Sadka (1978).
2. Roughly speaking, weak separability between $(c, n)$ and $b$ means that the indifference map for $c$ and $n$ does not depend on $b$; for a formal definition of weak separability, see Goldman and Uzawa (1964).
3. The issues of population growth and bequest as a public good within the family are also considered by Kemp and Leonard (1983).

4.  In most of the preceding analysis, investment played no central role, and, for the sake of notational simplicity, we generally assumed that $R = 1$. In this analysis, however, investment is a focus of our attention and thus we assume, more realistically, that $R \geq 1$.
5.  A more general specification of the model is to replace $c^2$ by $c^{2A}$ and $c^{2B}$ and to assume that $u$ is symmetric and quasiconcave in $c^{2A}$ and $c^{2B}$. In this case, the consumption of each child may be unequal, but the parent reveals a preference towards equality (see, e.g., Becker and Tomes, 1976, Sheshinski and Weiss, 1982). This more general specification will lead to equality of children's consumption only under special circumstances.
6.  Notice that our analysis proceeds on the assumption that the returns to various types of investment are known with certainty. If such returns are uncertain at the time investments are made, the case for a tax is strengthened. Such a tax reduces risk (Musgrave and Domar (1944); Eaton and Rosen (1980)) and thus improves the welfare of risk-adverse parents.
7.  A standard theorem in the theory of taxation is that a tax that is redistributed to the consumer in a lump sum is welfare-reducing (see, e.g., Diamond and McFadden (1974)).

# References

Becker, Gary S. (1976), "Altruism, Egoism and Genetic Fitness: Economics and Sociobiology." *Journal of Economic Literature*, **14**, 817–26.

Becker, Gary S. (1974). "A Theory of Social Interaction." *Journal of Political Economy*, **82**, 1063–1093.

Becker, G. S. and H. G. Lewis (1973), "On the Interaction between the Quantity and Quality of Children." *Journal of Political Economy*, **81**, 279–88.

Becker, Gary S., and Nigel Tomes (1976), "Child Endowments and the Quantity and Quality of Children." *Journal of Political Economy*, **84**, S142–63.

Bruno, Michael and Jack Habib (1976), "Taxes, Family Grants and Redistribution." *Journal of Public Economics*, **5**, 57–80.

Buchanan, J. and M. Kafoglis (1963), "A Note on Public Goods Supply." *American Economic Review*, **53**, 403–14.

Diamond, Peter A, and Daniel L. McFadden (1974), "Some Uses of the Expenditure Function in Public Finance." *Journal of Public Economics*, **3**, 3–21.

Diamond, Peter A, and J. A. Mirrlees, (1973), "Aggregate Production with Consumption Externalities." *Quarterly Journal of Economics*, **87**, 1–24.

Eaton, Jonathan, and Harvey S. Rosen (1980), "Taxation, Human Capital and Uncertainty." *American Economic Review*, **70**, 705–15.

Goldman, Steve, and Hirofumi Uzawa (1964), "A Note on Separability in Demand Analysis." *Econometrica*, **32**, 387–98.

Hirschleifer, J. (1977), "Shakespeare vs. Becker on Altruism: The Importance of Having the Last Word." *Journal of Economic Literature*, **15**, 500–2.

Kemp, M. C. and D. Leonard, (1983), "A Contribution to the Theory of Economic Planning: A Family-Based Model of Population Growth." Mimeo.

Musgrave, Richard A., and Evsey D. Domar (1944), "Proportional Income Taxation and Risk-Taking." *Quarterly Journal of Economics*, **58**, 387–422.

Sadka, Efraim (1978), "A Note on Aggregate Production with Consumption Externalities." *Journal of Public Economics*, **9**, 101–5.

Sheshinski, Eytan, and Yoram Weiss (1982), "Inequality within and between Families." *Journal of Political Economy*, **90**, 105–28.

# CHAPTER 9

# Children as a Capital Good

The "old age security hypothesis" essentially views children as a capital good. In the words of Schultz (1974), children are "the poor man's capital" in developing countries. Becker (1960) writes that "...it is possible that in the mid-nineteenth century children were a net producer's good, providing rather than using income." Neher (1971) and Willis (1980) develop the idea that parents in less-developed countries are motivated, in part, to bear and rear children because they expect children to care for them in old age. In particular, Willis develops a model in which output is assumed to be produced with labor alone; any consumption demand for children is ignored by assuming that parents' utility is solely a function of their own consumption of commodities and that transfers from their own children are parents only source of consumption in old age. Neher's assumptions are similar.

In this chapter we examine further the old age security hypothesis. A common conclusion of many writers is that better access to capital markets unambiguously reduces the demand for children, because children are less essential as a means of transferring income from the present to the future. For instance, Neher (1971) writes that "... the good asset (bonds) drives out the bad asset (children)." However, this conclusion does not always hold. There may be various reasons. Here we elaborate on two of them.

One reason lies in the microeconomics of fertility behavior. When child numbers and welfare enter parents' utility functions—the crucial feature of the analysis in this book—introduction of a capital market for transferring present to future consumption may plausibly increase the demand for children because a better access to capital markets increases welfare and thus may create a positive income effect on the desired number of children. This effect may dominate the negative substitution effect that a better access to capital markets may have on the number of children.

A second reason that the old age security hypothesis may not hold lies in the macroeconomic (general equilibrium) aspects of fertility and savings. The rate of interest that clears capital markets is endogenously determined: it may be higher than the rate of return on investment in children for some families, but it may be lower for other families. The latter are induced to borrow in order to invest in children. The overall effect of access to capital markets on the aggregate number of children is therefore ambiguous, depending on the balance of families.

## 1.  A Simple Model of the Old Age Security Hypothesis

Let parents live for two periods during which they consume $\bar{c}$ in the first period and $\tilde{c}$ in the second. Utility is assumed to be a function of only $\bar{c}$ and $\tilde{c}$, i.e., $u = u(\bar{c}, \tilde{c})$. All income is assumed to be produced by labor alone, and parents and children are assumed to receive an endowment per capita of $K_1$ and $K_2$, respectively, measured in units of consumption. As before, let $n$ be the number of children per family. Children are assumed to consume $x_1$ in the first period of life and $x_2$ in the second period when they are productive. For the moment, we consider $x_1$ and $x_2$ to be exogenously given (at conventional or subsistence levels). The difference between parents' consumption plus childrearing costs in the first period represents savings, $S$:

$$(9.1) \qquad\qquad K_1 = \bar{c} + S + nx_1, \qquad \bar{c}, S, n \geq 0.$$

In this model savings represent only a transfer via investment from period one to period two, and no borrowing from the future is possible. As before, suppose that such investment returns $R$ units of consumption of period two for every unit of consumption foregone in period one. Parents are assumed to earn nothing in period two and to subsist on transfers from their own children and returns from prior investment. Each child consumes only $x_2$

$(\leq K_2)$. Thus, parents' budget constraint in the second period is

$$(9.2) \qquad\qquad nK_2 + RS = \tilde{c} + nx_2, \qquad \tilde{c}, S, n \geq 0.$$

Suppose first that there is no capital market, so that $S = 0$, by definition, and children became the *sole* means of transferring consumption from the present to the future. In this case one can solve for $n$ from (9.1) and (9.2) to get

$$(a) \quad n = \frac{K_1 - \bar{c}}{x_1},$$

(9.3)

$$(b) \quad n = \frac{\tilde{c}}{K_2 - x_2}.$$

Equations (9.3a)–(9.3b) can also be used to solve for $\bar{c}$ and $\tilde{c}$ as functions of $n$:

$$(a) \quad \bar{c} = K_1 - nx_1,$$

(9.4)

$$(b) \quad \tilde{c} = n(K_2 - x_2).$$

One can view (9.4) as defining parametrically (via $n$) the consumption possibility frontier of the parents in $\bar{c} - \tilde{c}$ space. One can also substitute (9.3a) into (9.4b) to get the direct relationship between $\tilde{c}$ and $\bar{c}$:

$$(9.5) \qquad\qquad \tilde{c} = \frac{K_1(K_2 - x_2)}{x_1} - \frac{K_2 - x_2}{x_1}\bar{c}.$$

This consumption possibility frontier is depicted in Figure 9.1.

Parents choose the point on the consumption possibility frontier (9.5) that maximizes their utility function $u(\bar{c}, \tilde{c})$, point $(\bar{c}^*, \tilde{c}^*)$ in Figure 9.1. Once they find the optimal consumption bundle $(\bar{c}^*, \tilde{c}^*)$, the optimal number of children $n^*$ is determined from (9.3a) or (9.3b).

Observe that an increase in the cost of children, $x_1$, reduces the slope of the budget line in Figure 9.1 and the intercept with the vertical axis, leaving unchanged the intercept with the horizontal axis. Therefore, if $\tilde{c}$ is not a Giffen good, then $\tilde{c}$ falls and, by (9.3b), $n$ also falls. However, the effect of a decrease in the return from investment in children $(K_2 - x_2)$ on the number of children is ambiguous. Such a change has the same effect on the budget line as before (making $\tilde{c}$ more expensive relative to $\bar{c}$) and again, $\tilde{c}$ must fall if it is not a Giffen good. However, whether $n$ falls or rises depends on whether the decrease in $\tilde{c}$ is proportionally higher or lower than the decrease in $(K_2 - x_2)$; see (9.3b) since the return to their investment through children falls, families may need to invest more (i.e., have more children) even if they are

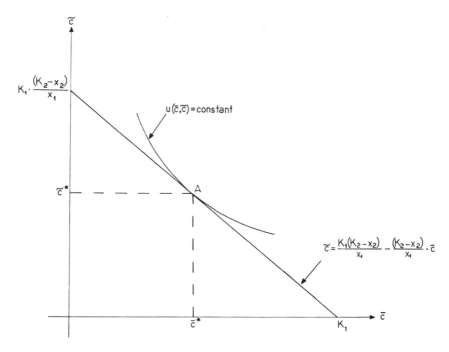

**Figure 9.1.** Consumption Possibility Frontier for Parents Transferring Resources to Period 2 via Their Children.

content with consuming less in the future. In contrast, an increase in the parents' endowment, $K_1$, has a pure income effect. The consumption possibility frontier shifts upward without any change in its slope; $\tilde{c}$ increases if it is a normal good and thus, by (9.3b), the number of children $n$, must also rise.

In general, families differ in the amounts of endowment parents have ($K_1$) and can expect their children to have ($K_2$). Both affect the number of children desired, but differences in the latter affect the rate of return on investment in children, so that, if an alternative means of transferring present to future consumption, such as capital market, is available, the total number of children as well as their distribution among families may change.

If a capital market exists, in the sense of an alternative means (to children) for transferring present to future consumption, $S$ may be strictly positive for some families. In this case, (9.1) and (9.2) may be consolidated by substituting for $S$ in (9.2) from (9.1):

(9.6) $$K_1 + \left[ \frac{K_2 - x_2}{R} - x_1 \right] n = \bar{c} + \frac{\tilde{c}}{R},$$

with an added requirement that $S = K_1 - \bar{c} - nx_1 \geq 0$. The expression in square brackets is the net present value of having a child. It consists of a return $(K_2 - X_2)$ in the future, which is worth only $(K_2 - X_2)/R$ in the present, and a cost, $x_1$, in the present. Clearly, since $n$ does not enter the utility function, a family will have children only if

$$(9.7) \qquad \frac{K_2 - x_2}{R} \geq x_1.$$

Thus, in the presence of a capital market, those families for whom $x_1$ or $x_2$ is sufficiently high will have no children and will transfer present to future consumption via the capital market. Families for whom the expected endowments of their children are sufficiently low may also choose to have no children. Those families for whom the rate of return on investment in children is sufficiently high will not save at all: they will hit the constraint $S = K_1 - \bar{c} - nx_1 \geq 0$ as they try to increase $n$. Consequently, they will be subject to exactly the same constraint as in the absence of a capital market, i.e., equation (9.3), and will demand the same number of children. Since some families will have no children, total population must be lower than without a capital market. This analysis is the essence of the old age security hypothesis.

## 2. The Old Age Security Hypothesis Reconsidered: A Microeconomic Analysis

The preceding discussion assumed that neither numbers of children nor children's welfare enter parents' utility function. However, if parents do care about their children, which is an essential ingredient of our approach, there is no presumption that the existence of a capital market will lead to a lesser demand for children than in its absence.

Suppose that the utility function is

$$(9.8) \qquad u(\bar{c}, \tilde{c}, x_1, x_2, n),$$

so that parents care about the number of their children, $n$, and their children's welfare, which, in turn, depends on the children's consumption, $x_1$ and $x_2$. Parents now choose $x_1$ and $x_2$ as well as $n$, $\bar{c}$, and $\tilde{c}$.

In the absence of a capital market, parents choose $\bar{c}$, $\tilde{c}$, $x_1$, $x_2$, $n$ so as to maximize (9.8) subject to (9.1) and (9.2), where $S$ is set equal to zero. With a capital market, they are not constrained to have $S$ equal to 0. Comparing the optimal $n$ in these two cases does not yield an unambiguous result. Some insight into the source of this ambiguity may be obtained by assuming that children are born in the second period (i.e., $x_1 = 0$) and $u$ is weakly separable between $(\tilde{c}, x_2, n)$ and $\bar{c}$ (see Goldman and Uzawa (1964) for a definition and discussion of weak separability). That is, $u$ can be written as

(9.9) $$u(\bar{c}, \tilde{c}, x_2, n) = f(\bar{c}, v(\tilde{c}, x_2, n)).$$

In this case $\tilde{c}$, $x_2$, and $n$ must maximize $v(\cdot)$ subject to the second-period budget constraint, $RS = \tilde{c} + nx_2 - nK_2$. Thus, one can see that the difference between the optimal $\tilde{c}$, $x_2$, and $n$ in the absence of a capital market ($S = 0$) and in the presence of a capital market ($S > 0$) results only from an income effect.

Observe that $x_2$ may be interpreted as the "quality" of children, as in the work of Becker and Lewis (1973), (further elaborated on in Chapter 5, above). $K_2$ plays the same role as a child allowance in the earlier chapters of this book. As we noted above, quality is part of the "price" of a unit of the quantity of children and, conversely, quantity is the "price" of a unit of the quality. Since these "prices" are control variables (controlled by parents), the income effect in this household optimization problem is coupled with an endogenous price effect. As we illustrate in Chapter 5, no unambiguous conclusion can be reached about the effect of an increase in income on the quality of children.

We establish in Chapter 5 conditions on certain demand elasticities that guarantee that income has a negative effect on the quantity of children. In this case the old age security hypothesis may indeed hold. However, this result is indeed special. In general, if $x_1 \neq 0$, if the weak separability assumption does not hold, or if the aforementioned elasticity conditions are not satisfied, then the introduction of a capital market may well cause an increase in the number of children.

For example, maintain the weak separability assumption and make $x_1 = 0$. If the elasticities of substitution between $\tilde{c}$ and $x_2$ and between $x_2$ and $n$ are sufficiently low and if a family is induced to save by the introduction of a capital market, that family will also increase $\tilde{c}$, $x_2$, and $n$. For example, consider the extreme case in which the elasticities of substitution between $\tilde{c}$ and $x_2$ and between $x_2$ and $n$ are zero. In this case the utility function (9.9) is written as

$$u(\bar{c}, \tilde{c}, x_2, n) = f(\bar{c}, \min\{\tilde{c}, \gamma x_2, \delta n\})$$

for some $\gamma > 0$ and $\delta > 0$.

Clearly, the parents choose to have $\tilde{c} = \gamma x_2 = \delta n$ in this case. For those families who continue not to save after the introduction of a capital market, $n$ will be unchanged. However, all three variables—$\tilde{c}$, $x_2$, and $n$—increase in the same proportion if there is saving. The old age security hypothesis is thus invalid.

## 3.   The Old Age Security Hypothesis Reconsidered: A General Equilibrium Example

In the preceding section, the general validity of the old age security hypothesis was shown to be invalid under the assumption that parents care about their children. Indeed, the hypothesis does not hold in a general equilibrium framework even when parents do not care about their children. In this section we return to the assumptions of Section 1, in which parents view their children only as a capital good and show that the introduction of a capital market (i.e., the possibility of lending and borrowing) may plausibly lead to a larger population when the interest factor $(R)$ is endogenously determined so as to clear the capital market.

Suppose that the utility function, which depends only on $\bar{c}$ and $\tilde{c}$, is of the Cobb-Douglas form,

$$(9.10) \qquad u(\bar{c}, \tilde{c}) = \bar{c}^{\alpha}\tilde{c}^{1-\alpha}.$$

Suppose also that there are only two types of families, $A$ and $B$, of equal numbers with the same preferences (as described by (9.10)); the same endowments, $K_1$ and $K_2$; the same second-period child consumption, $x_2$; but different first-period child-costs, $x_1^A$ and $x_1^B$. Assume that $x_1^A > x_1^B$, so that the return on investment in children (namely, $(K_2 - x_2)/x_1$) is higher for a $B$ family than for an $A$ family.

In the absence of a capital market, $S$ is equal to zero and the relevant budget constraint (9.5) is

$$\tilde{c} = \frac{K_1(K_2 - x_2)}{x_1^i} - \frac{K_2 - x_2}{x_1^i}\bar{c}, \qquad i = A, B.$$

Maximizing the utility function (9.10) subject to this budget constraint yields

$$(9.11) \qquad \begin{array}{l} \text{(a)} \quad \bar{c}^i = \alpha K_1, \\[2ex] \text{(b)} \quad \tilde{c}^i = \dfrac{(1-\alpha)K_1(K_2 - x_2)}{x_1^i}, \end{array}$$

where $i = A, B$. Employing (9.3),

$$(9.12) \qquad n^i = \frac{(1-\alpha)K_1}{x_1^i}, \qquad i = A, B.$$

that is, the family with the higher $x_1$ has a smaller number of children. The aggregate number of children in this case can be found from (9.12):

$$(9.13) \qquad N^* = (1-\alpha)K_1\left(\frac{1}{x_1^A} + \frac{1}{x_1^B}\right).$$

Appropriate modification can be made for unequal numbers of family types.

Now, let us introduce the possibility of both lending ($S > 0$) and borrowing ($S < 0$) via a competitive capital market. In this case, the budget constraint (9.6) becomes

$$K_1 + \left[\frac{K_2 - x_2}{R} - x_1^i\right]n = \bar{c} + \frac{\tilde{c}}{R}, \qquad i = A, B,$$

*without* the added requirement that $S = K_1 - \bar{c} - nx_1^i \geq 0$. From this budget constraint, it is evident that, if the rate of return on investment in children for some family exceeds the market rate of interest, namely,

$$\frac{K - x_2}{x_1^i} > R,$$

it pays that family to borrow indefinitely and increase the number of children indefinitely; this situation cannot be an equilibrium. Thus, at equilibrium, the interest rate cannot fall short of the rate of return on investment in children for any family: thus,

(9.14)                     $$R \geq \frac{K_2 - x_2}{x_1^B} > \frac{K_2 - x_2}{x_1^A}.$$

Now, if the first inequality in (9.14) is strict, both types of families have zero demand for children (because the rate of return on investment in children is lower than the rate of interest). In this case, both types of families will want to save, since it is the only way to have a positive level of second-period consumption, which is essential given the Cobb-Douglas specification of the utility function. But when both types of families save, there cannot be a capital market equilibrium. Thus, at equilibrium,

(9.15)                     $$R = \frac{K_2 - x_2}{x_1^B} > \frac{K_2 - x_2}{x_1^A}.$$

In this case, a family of type $A$ has a zero demand for children,

(9.16)                                   $$n^A = 0,$$

while $\bar{c}^A$ and $\tilde{c}^A$ are given by

(9.17)
$$\text{(a)} \quad \bar{c}^A = \alpha K_1$$
$$\text{(b)} \quad \tilde{c}^A = (1 - \alpha)K_1 R = \frac{(1 - \alpha)K_1(K_2 - x_2)}{x_1^B}.$$

The saving of a family of type $A$, which is $K_1 - \bar{c}^A$, is given by

(9.18)                               $$S^A = (1 - \alpha)K_1.$$

A family of type $B$ is indifferent between investing in the capital market and investing in children (because $(K_2 - x_2)/x_1^B = R$). The consumption of this type of family in the first and second periods is given by:

(9.19)

$$\text{(a)} \quad \bar{c}^B = \alpha K_1,$$

$$\text{(b)} \quad \bar{c}^B = (1 - \alpha)K_1 R = \frac{(1 - \alpha)K_1(K_2 - x_2)}{x_1^B}.$$

Given equilibrium in the capital market,

(9.20)

$$S^B = -S^A = -(1 - \alpha)K_1.$$

In order to find $n^B$, substitute (9.19a) and (9.20) into the first-period budget constraint (9.1) to obtain

(9.21)

$$n^B = \frac{K_1 - \bar{c}^B - S^B}{x_1^B} = \frac{2(1 - \alpha)K_1}{x_1^B}.$$

The aggregate number of children in this case is found from (9.16) and (9.21) when the numbers of type $A$ and type $B$ families are the same:

(9.22)

$$N^{**} = n^A + n^B = \frac{2(1 - \alpha)K_1}{x_1^B}.$$

Comparing $N^*$ and $N^{**}$, (9.13) and (9.22), one can see that

$$N^{**} = \frac{2(1 - \alpha)K_1}{x_1^B} = (1 - \alpha)K_1\left(\frac{1}{x_1^B} + \frac{1}{x_1^B}\right)$$

$$> (1 - \alpha)K_1\left(\frac{1}{x_1^A} + \frac{1}{x_1^B}\right) = N^*.$$

Of course, this conclusion holds only if the relative numbers of the two types of families are the same. Appropriate modifications can be made for unequal numbers of family types.

Thus, in a general equilibrium framework, the introduction of a capital market *increases* rather than decreases the number of children, contrary to the old age security hypothesis. In the absence of a capital market, both types of families transfer resources from the present to the future via children. With a capital market, only families with the higher rate of return on children use this means of transferring resources from the present to the future. In the case we examined, the economy uses only the more efficient investment in children, and the aggregate investment in them is greater.

## References

Becker, G. S. (1960), "An Economic Analysis of Fertility," In R. Easterlin (ed.), *Demographic and Economic Change in Developing Countries.* Princeton: Princeton University Press.

Becker, G. S. and H. G. Lewis (1973), "On the Interaction between the Quantity and Quality of Children." *Journal of Political Economy,* **81**, 279–288.

Goldman, S. and H. Uzawa (1964), "A Note on Separability in Demand Analysis." *Econometrica,* **32**, 387–98.

Neher, P. A. (1971), "Peasants, Procreation and Pensions." *American Economic Review,* **61**, 380–389.

Schultz, T. W. (1974), ed., *Economics of the Family: Marriage, Children and Human Capital.* Chicago and London: NBER.

Willis, R. J. (1980), "The Old Age Security Hypothesis and Population Growth," in T. Burch, ed., *Demographic Behavior: Interdisciplinary Perspectives on Decision Making.* Boulder: Westview Press.

CHAPTER **10**

# Intragenerational Income Distribution Policies

We have dealt so far only with *intergenerational* issues of efficiency and equity. We turn now to a discussion of some aspects of *intragenerational* issues with endogenous fertility and labor supply.

Since Schultz (1974), it has been widely recognized that fertility and labor supply interact in an important way: It is not possible to analyze female labor force participation rates taking the number and age distribution of children in the family as exogenous, nor it is possible to model adequately parents' choices with respect to the number and spacing of their children when the mother's participation decision is taken as given. That endogenous fertility has important implications for other intragenerational issues, such as the determination of family equivalence scales in demand analysis or optimal taxation policy in public finance, is less widely appreciated. Deaton and Muellbauer (1983), writing on the welfare implications of family size and age composition for income inequality, base their results on an analysis of consumption expenditures in which the numbers of children in the family and their ages are taken as given. For the most part, the literature on optimal taxation policy ignores family size and composition entirely (e.g., Mirrlees, 1971, 1976; Sadka, 1976); those studies that take family size into account treat it as exogenous (e.g., Mirrlees, 1976; Bruno and Habib, 1976; Balcer and Sadka, 1982).[1] Of course, the descriptive literature on tax policy deals extensively with the treatment of family size in taxation systems (e.g., Musgrave, 1959; Pechman, 1966).

In this chapter we analyze the implications of endogenous fertility for intragenerational welfare comparisons of alternative policies with respect to income taxation and family allowances. Considering that nearly every system of taxation either makes some provision for differences in family size and composition or has provisions that have varying welfare implications depending on such differences, the apparent lack of attention in the theoretical literature to the implications of endogenous fertility is surprising. Tax and family policies designed to affect the distribution of income or welfare that do not take into account their effects on fertility may have unintended consequences. For example, if poverty, in the sense of low family income per capita, tends to be associated with large family size, a system of child allowances and tax exemptions designed to alleviate poverty and reduce inequality may actually worsen the situation.

Throughout this chapter, it is assumed that preferences are given and homogenous. However, there are differences in (exogenous) opportunities such as innate abilities that induce differences in income or welfare and, since fertility is endogenous, such differences in opportunities also induce differences in family size. In Section 1 we assume that labor supply is given; this assumption is relaxed in Section 2. The pure effects on fertility are isolated in the model of Section 1, in which we consider a very simple tax system depending only on family size; more complicated tax systems are considered in Section 2, in which the fertility effects are complicated by endogenously variable income resulting from variable labor supply. Since we focus in this chapter on intragenerational redistribution, we use a social welfare function that depends directly on the utilities of existing parents only. The welfare of children enters the social welfare function only through the welfare of parents who care about their children.

## 1. Fixed Labor Supply

Consider an economy with families who have identical tastes but different (exogenous) incomes. For the sake of simplicity, we assume that families have only two income levels ($K^1$ and $K^2$, where $K^1 < K^2$). In this chapter it is more convenient to work with the variable $q$, which is total expenditure on children (rather than per-capita expenditure). (The advantages of this approach are explained in Chapter 5.) Thus, parents' utility function is written as

$$(10.1) \qquad\qquad U(c, q, n),$$

where $c$ is parents' consumption and $n$ is, as before, the number of children.

The government in this economy uses a child allowance, $\beta$, which may be either positive or negative, and it balances its budget by imposing a uniform lump-sum tax ($T$) on each household. Thus, the tax system in this economy is a function only of family size.[2]

The budget constraint of a household with income $K_i$ ($i = 1, 2$) is therefore

$$(10.2) \qquad\qquad c + q - \beta n \leq K^i - T.$$

The household chooses $c$, $q$, and $n$ so as to maximize the utility function (10.1), subject to the budget constraint (10.2), which yields an indirect utility function $V(K^i - T, \beta)$ and demand functions $C(K^i - T, \beta)$, $Q(K^i - T, \beta)$, and $N(K^i - T, \beta)$ for consumption, total child expenditure, and number of children, respectively. Observe that since tastes are the same for all households, the above functions are the same for all households, except, of course, that their arguments can take different values for different households.

Using the envelope theorem (see the appendix to Chapter 4), one can derive Roy's identity for endogenous fertility:

$$(10.3) \qquad\qquad V_2 = NV_1.$$

A critical assumption of this chapter is that poverty and family size are positively associated, i.e.,

$$(10.4) \qquad\qquad N_1 < 0.$$

(This assumption was discussed in detail in Chapter 5.) Observe that the assumption refers to the reduced form demand function for number of children and, as explained in Chapter 5, it does not necessarily imply that children are inferior in the usual sense. Specifically, if one defines $z = q/n$ as the quality per child, the budget constraint can be written as $c + zn = K$ (ignoring the government's instruments, $T$ and $\beta$). With this rewriting of the budget constraint, it is clear that $z$ is the "price" of $n$ and vice versa (see Chapter 5). Assumption (10.4) is perfectly consistent with the assumption that $n$ is a normal good in the usual sense: If one defines an artificial household optimization problem

$$(10.5) \quad \max_{c, z, n} (\bar{U}(c, z, n) \equiv U(c, zn, n)) \quad \text{such that} \quad c + p_n n + p_z z = K,$$

then assumption (10.4) is perfectly compatible with the assumption that an increase in income $K$ in (10.5) leads to a larger $n$. The difference between the artificial problem (10.5) and the *true* household optimization problem (max $\bar{U}(c, z, n)$, subject to $c + zn = K$) is that in the former the price of $n$ (namely, $p_n$) is kept constant, while in the latter the price of $n$ (namely, $z$) is not kept constant. This difference is why in the true problem $n$ may plausibly fall with income. In fact, Becker and Lewis (1973) establish plausible conditions under which assumption (10.4) holds, which are also derived in Chapter 5.

The government budget constraint is given by

$$(10.6) \qquad 2T - \beta[N(K^1 - T, \beta) + N(K^2 - T, \beta)] \geq 0.$$

The government wishes to maximize an individualistic social welfare function $W(V(K^1 - T, \beta), V(K^2 - T, \beta))$, with $W_1 > 0$ and $W_2 > 0$. In general, $W$ may be written (locally) as a weighted average of the two utility functions. Here we analyze only the two polar cases in which all the weight is assigned to either the first type of family or the second type of family.

The government does not use individual-specific taxes or subsidies, but this does not mean that the government is not engaged in redistributing income from the small rich families to the large poor families or vice versa. In fact, a positive child alowance redistributes income from small rich families to large poor families. But since each family can choose whether to be large or small in size, the poor household (i.e., the household with pretax income $K^1$) will always be worse off than the rich household (i.e., the household with pretax income $K^2$). Hence it is always true that

$$V(K^1 - T, \beta) < V(K^2 - T, \beta),$$

because, by assumption, $K^1 < K^2$, and $V(\cdot, \cdot)$ is strictly increasing in its first argument.

Thus, our two polar cases correspond to the Rawlsian max-min social welfare criterion and to the max-max social welfare criterion. All the other cases and the results corresponding to them are intermediate between the two polar cases.

In order to simplify, we use the following notation

$$v^i \text{ for } V(K^i - T, \beta),$$
$$c^i \text{ for } C(K^i - T, \beta),$$
$$q^i \text{ for } Q(K^i - T, \beta),$$

and

$$n^i \text{ for } N(K^i - T, \beta),$$

where $i = 1, 2$. A similar notation is used for the partial derivatives of the functions $V$, $C$, $Q$, and $N$:

$$v_j^i \equiv V_j(K^i - T, \beta),$$
$$c_j^i \equiv C_j(K^i - T, \beta),$$
$$q_j^i \equiv Q_j(K^i - T, \beta),$$

and

$$n_j^i \equiv N_j(K^i - T, \beta),$$

where $j = 1, 2$.

### 1.a. A Max-min Social Welfare Function

The social objective is to choose $T$ and $\beta$ so as to maximize the welfare of the poor family, $V(K^1 - T, \beta)$, subject to the government's revenue constraint (10.6). The first-order conditions are:

(10.7′) $$-v_1^1 + 2\lambda + \lambda\beta(n_1^1 + n_1^2) = 0,$$

(10.8′) $$v_2^1 - \lambda(n^1 + n^2) - \lambda\beta(n_2^1 + n_2^2) = 0,$$

where $\lambda > 0$ is the Lagrange multiplier associated with the government's budget constraint (10.6). Multiplying (10.7′) by $n^1$ and using (10.3), which states that $v_2^1 = n^1 v_1^1$, one obtains

(10.9) $$-v_2^1 + 2\lambda n^1 + \lambda n^1 \beta(n_1^1 + n_1^2) = 0.$$

Adding (10.9) to (10.8′) yields (after dividing by $\lambda$)

(10.10′) $$(1 + \beta n_1^2)(n^1 - n^2) = \beta(n_2^1 - n^1 n_1^1) + \beta(n_2^2 - n^2 n_1^2).$$

Observe that the only *exogenous* difference between the two families is in income $(K^1 < K^2)$. They have the same tastes and are subject to the same tax subsidy parameters, $T$ and $\beta$. Therefore, by assumption (10.4), the poorer family will have more children. Thus,

(10.11) $$n^1 - n^2 > 0.$$

Again using the envelope theorem, note that an increase in $\beta$ changes the real income of family $i$ by $n^i$. Thus, the term $n_2^i - n^i n_1^i$ is the Hicks-compensated derivative of $n^i$ with respect to $\beta$ (see Chapters 4 and 5). Since $\beta$ is a subsidy to the number of children, it follows from the properties of the Hicks-Slutsky substitution matrix that

(10.12) $$n_2^i - n^i n_1^i > 0, \qquad i = 1, 2.$$

Rewriting the family budget constraint (10.2) as

$$c + q = K - T + \beta n,$$

it follows that

(10.13)                         $$\frac{\partial(C + Q)}{\partial(K - T)} \equiv C_1 + Q_1 = 1 + \beta N_1.$$

Assuming that total expenditure of the family, namely $C + Q$, is a normal good, it follows from (10.13) that

(10.14)                         $$1 + \beta n_1^i > 0, \qquad i = 1, 2.$$

Using (10.11), (10.12), and (10.14), one concludes from the first-order condition (10.10') that $\beta > 0$. Thus, a max-min optimal policy calls for a positive child allowance.

## 1.b.   A Max-max Social Welfare Function

Replacing the objective function $V(K^1 - T, \beta)$ of the preceding sub-section by $V(K^2 - T, \beta)$, the analogue of first order conditions (10.7') and (10.8') are

(10.7'')                        $$-v_1^2 + 2\lambda + \lambda\beta(n_1^1 + n_1^2) = 0,$$

and

(10.8'')                        $$v_2^2 - \lambda(n^1 + n^2) - \lambda\beta(n_2^1 + n_2^2) = 0.$$

Using the same procedures as in the preceding subsection, one can derive from (10.7'') and (10.8'') the analogue of (10.10'):

(10.10'')     $$(1 + \beta n_1^1)(n^2 - n^1) = \beta(n_2^1 - n^1 n_1^1) + \beta(n_2^2 - n^2 n_1^2).$$

Using (10.11), (10.12), and (10.14), one concludes that $\beta < 0$. Thus, a max-max optimal policy calls for a positive tax on children.

So far we have assumed that richer families have fewer children (10.4). If this assumption is reversed, namely, that $N_1 > 0$ (see Chapter 5 for a discussion of when this is the case), then our policy recommendations must also be reversed: a max-min optimal policy leads to a positive tax on children, and a max-max policy leads to a positive child allowance. In all other intermediate cases, including the Benthamite sum-of-utilities of the *existing* parents, the optimal $\beta$ may be of either sign.

In this section we have assumed that labor supply is perfectly inelastic. However, what is essential for our results to hold is not the inelasticity of the labor supply but rather the absence of a distortionary wage tax. In the next section, we introduce leisure into the utility function, and it is straightforward to show that the same results hold if wage income is not taxed. If wage income is taxed, then whether $\beta$ is positive or negative depends on the nature of the substitutability between leisure and number of children.

## 2. A Model with Variable Labor Supply

In this case, let utility depend also on leisure, which varies inversely with labor services ($l$). The utility function (10.1) now becomes

$$(10.15) \qquad\qquad U(c, q, n, l),$$

where $U_4 < 0$, i.e., there is a disutility of labor. In addition to assuming identical tastes of families, we assume different abilities, which are reflected in the wage rates. Income is now no longer exogenous. Specifically, a poor family can earn a wage rate of $w^1$, and a rich family can earn a wage rate of $w^2$, where $w^1 < w^2$. In addition to a child allowance, $\beta$, we assume that the government imposes a linear income tax with a marginal rate, $t$, and a lump-sum tax $T$ (per family, not per capita).[3] The budget constraint of household $i$ is now

$$(10.16) \qquad c + q - \beta n \leq w^i(1 - t)l - T, \qquad i = 1, 2.$$

A maximization of the utility function (10.15) subject to the budget constraint (10.16) gives rise to the indirect utility function $V(-T, \beta, w^i(1 - t))$ with demand functions $C(-T, \beta, w^i(1 - t))$, $N(-T, \beta, w^i(1 - t))$, and $Q(-T, \beta, w^i(1 - t))$ for consumption, quantity of children, and total child expenditures, respectively, and to the labor supply function $L(-T, \beta, w^i(1 - t))$. As in the preceding section, these functions are the same for all households although the values of their arguments differ across households. We continue to follow the convenient practice of using $v^i$ for $V(-T, \beta, w^i(1 - t))$, $n_j^i$ for $N_j(-T, \beta, w^i(1 - t))$, etc.

Roy's identities (see Chapter 4) are now

$$(10.17) \qquad\qquad V_2 = NV_1, \qquad V_3 = LV_1.$$

The government's budget constraint becomes

$$(10.18) \quad t[w^1 L(-T, \beta, w^1(1 - t)) + w^2 L(-T, \beta, w^2(1 - t))]$$
$$+ 2T - \beta[N(-T, \beta, w^1(1 - t)) + N(-T, \beta, w^2(1 - t))] \geq 0.$$

The government chooses, $t$, $T$, and $\beta$ so as to maximize an individualistic social welfare function $W(V(-T, \beta, w^1(1 - t)), V(-T, \beta, w^2(1 - t)))$, subject to the budget constraint (10.18). As before, we consider the two polar cases of max-min and max-max social welfare functions.

## 2.a.  A Max-min Social Welfare Function

The government in this case maximizes $v(-T, \beta, w^1(1-t))$ subject to its budget constraint (10.18). The first-order conditions are

(10.19)         $-v_1^1 + 2\lambda + \lambda\beta(n_1^1 + n_1^2) - \lambda t(w^1 l_1^1 + w^2 l_1^2) = 0,$

(10.20)      $v_2^1 - \lambda(n^1 + n^2) - \lambda\beta(n_2^1 + n_2^2) + \lambda t(w^1 l_2^1 + w^2 l_2^2) = 0$

and

(10.21)                $-v_3^1 w^1 + \lambda\beta(n_3^1 w^1 + n_3^2 w^2) + \lambda(w^1 l^1 + w^2 l^2)$

$$- \lambda t[(w^1)^2 l_3^1 + (w^2)^2 l_3^2] = 0,$$

where $\lambda > 0$ is a Langrangian multiplier.

Multiplying (10.19) by $n^1$ and adding the product to (10.20) to get

(10.22)   $[(n_2^1 - n^1 n_1^1) + (n_2^2 - n^2 n_1^2)]\beta - [w^1(l_2^1 - n^1 l_1^1) + w^2(l_2^2 - n^2 l_1^2)]t$

$$= (1 + \beta n_1 - twl_1)(n^1 - n^2),$$

use is made of Roy's identities (10.17). Similarly, multiplying (10.19) by $-w^1 l^1$ and adding the product to (10.21) to get

(10.23)   $-[w^1(n_3^1 - l^1 n_1^1)$

$$+ w^2(n_3^2 - l^2 n_1^2)]\beta + [(w^1)^2(l_3^1 - l^1 l_1^1) + (w^2)^2(l_3^2 - l^2 l_1^2)]t$$

$$= (1 + \beta n_1^2 - tw^2 l_1^2)(w^2 l^2 - w^1 l^1),$$

where use is again made of Roy's identities (10.17).

Under suitable assumptions, one can sign the terms comprising the system of the modified first-order conditions (10.22)–(10.23). First, consider the term $(n^1 - n^2)$. As in the preceding section, we can show that it is positive. Write $N_3$ as

(10.24)                         $N_3 = (N_3 - LN_1) + LN_1.$

Observe that $N_3 - LN_1$ is the Hicks-compensated derivative of $N$ with respect to the net wage, $(1 - t)w$ (see Chapters 4 and 5). Because a compensated increase in the net wage reduces leisure and since it is plausible to assume that children are time-intensive (i.e., children and leisure are complements), we assume that $N_3 - LN_1 < 0$. We continue to assume that $N_1 < 0$ (condition (10.4)), i.e., that income has a negative effect on the number of children. Thus, it follows from (10.24) that $N_3 < 0$. Since $(1 - t)w^1 < (1 - t)w^2$, we conclude that

(10.25)                                 $n^1 - n^2 > 0.$

Second, continue to assume that total expenditure of the family, namely, $C + Q$, is a normal good. Suppose also that leisure is a normal good (i.e., that $L_1 < 0$); then

(10.26)   $0 < C_1 + Q_1 = 1 + \beta N_1 + w(1 - t)L_1 < 1 + \beta N_1 - twL_1.$

Thus, it follows from (10.26) that

(10.27)                    $1 + \beta n_1^i - tw^i l_1^i > 0, \qquad i = 1, 2.$

Third, assume that the labor supply curve is not backward-bending. Hence, the more productive household works harder:

(10.28)                    $w^2 l^2 - w^1 l^1 > 0.$

Fourth, observe that $L_2 - NL_1$ is the Hicks-compensated derivative of the labor supply function with respect to $\beta$. By symmetry of the Hicks-Slutsky effects, $L_2 - NL_1$ is equal to the Hicks-compensated derivative of the quantity-of-children demand function with respect to the wage rate, i.e., $N_3 - LN_1$, which was assumed to be negative. Thus,

(10.29)              $l_2^i - n^i l_1^i = n_3^i - l^i n_1^i < 0, \qquad i = 1, 2.$

Fifth, as before, $N_2 - NN_1$ is the Hicks-compensated derivative of $N$ with respect to $\beta$. Thus,

(10.30)                    $n_2^i - n^i n_1^i > 0, \qquad i = 1, 2.$

Finally, $L_3 - LL_1$ is positive since it is the Hicks-compensated derivative of the labor supply function with respect to the wage rate. Thus,

(10.31)                    $l_3^i - l^i l_1^i > 0, \qquad i = 1, 2.$

The right-hand sides of the system (10.22)–(10.23) are both positive, by (10.25), (10.27), and (10.28). Also, the terms multiplying $\beta$ and $t$ on the left-hand sides of the system are all positive, by (10.29), (10.30), and (10.31). Thus, $\beta$ and $t$ cannot both be negative.

*Proposition 1.*   In the max-min case, at least one of the pair $(\beta, t)$ must be positive.

The rationale of this result is quite straightforward: Both the child allowance and the wage tax redistribute income from the rich to the poor; if both are negative, the government will be doing the opposite, i.e., redistributing income from the poor to the rich, which is inconsistent with the egalitarian objective of max-min.

Of course, our proposition does not rule out the possibility that either $\beta$ or $t$ will be negative. Of particular interest is the case in which $t$ is negative (of course, $\beta$ in this case will be positive), since negative $t$ is in contrast to the common result in the optimal income tax literature in which it is shown that a wage subsidy is not desirable. In order to see the various possibilities about the signs of $\beta$ and $t$, one can apply Cramer's rule to the system (10.22)–(10.23) in order to obtain

(10.32)
$$\beta = \frac{1 + \beta n_1^2 - tw^2 l_1^2}{D} \{(n^1 - n^2)[(w^1)^2(l_3^1 - l^1 l_1^1)$$

$$+ (w^2)^2(l_3^2 - l^2 l_1^2)] + (w^2 l^2 - w^1 l^1)[w^1(l_2^1 - n^1 l_1^1)$$

$$+ w^2(l_2^2 - n^2 l_1^2)]\},$$

and

(10.33)
$$t = \frac{1 + \beta n_1^2 - tw^2 l_1^2}{D} \{(n^1 - n^2)[w^1(n_3^1 - l n_1^1)$$

$$+ w^2(n_3^2 - l^2 n_1^2)] + (w^2 l^2 - w^1 l^1)[(n_2^1 - n^1 n_1^1)$$

$$+ (n_2^2 - n^2 n_1^2)]\},$$

where $D$ is the determinant of the system (10.22)–(10.23):

(10.34)
$$D = \det \sum_{i=1}^{2} \begin{pmatrix} n_2^i - n^i n_1^i & w^i(l_2^i - n^i l_1^i) \\ w^i(n_3^i - l^i n_1^i) & (w^i)^2(l_3^i - l^i l_1^i) \end{pmatrix}.$$

Observe that the matrices in (10.34) are nothing else but principal minors of the Hicks-Slutsky substitution matrices, except that the second row and the second column are each multiplied by the scalar $w^i > 0$. Since the Hicks-Slutsky matrix is negative semidefinite, its $2 \times 2$ principal minors have positive determinants. Hence, $D > 0$.

It is clear from (10.32)–(10.33) that the own-substitution and the cross-substitution effects work in opposite directions: the own-substitution effects tend to make $\beta$ and $t$ positive while the cross effects tend to make them negative. There are three possibilities. First, if the cross-substitution effect between leisure and number of children vanishes (i.e., $n_3^i - l^i n_1^i = l_2^i - n^i l_1^i = 0$) or is very small, the own-substitution effect dominates and both $\beta$ and $t$ are positive. Second, if the cross-substitution effect is large, $w^2 l^2 - w^1 l^1$ is relatively small, and $n^1 - n^2$ is relatively large, a positive $\beta$ is more effective than a positive $t$ in redistributing income from rich to poor families. If, in addition, the own-substitution effect of the child allowance on the number of children (namely, $n_2^i - n^i n_1^i$) is small relative to the own-substitution effect of the wage on the labor supply (namely, $l_3^i - l^i l_1^i$), $\beta$ is also less distortionary than $t$. (Note that the distortions created by $\beta$ on $L$ and by $t$ on $N$ are the same by the symmetry of the cross-substitution effects). In this case, $\beta$ will be positive and $t$ will be negative. Third, under opposite assumptions regarding the relative sizes of $w^2 l^2 - w^1 l^1$, $n^1 - n^2$, and the own-substitution effects, $\beta$ will be negative and $t$ will be positive.

### 2.b. *A Max-max Social Welfare Function*

The analysis of the max-max case is exactly analogous to that for max-min.

*Proposition 2.* In the max-max case, at least one of the pair $(\beta, t)$ must be negative.

Also in a complete analogy to the preceding subsection, both $\beta$ and $t$ are negative when the cross-substitution effects vanish, while otherwise one of them could be positive.

In all other intermediate cases between the max-min and the max-max, including the Benthamite sum-of-utilities of the existing parents, the sign of the optimal $\beta$ and $t$ cannot be determined a priori.

## Notes

1. Mirrlees (1972) is an exception.
2. Since income is exogenous, a nonlinear tax on income may be used to achieve any Pareto-optimal allocation. Similarly, if the government can impose proportional tax on income in addition to $T$, it can achieve perfect equality between the two types of families by taxing away all the exogenous income (a 100 percent marginal tax rate), and redistributing the proceeds equally (using a negative $T$). We analyze these more general tax systems in the next section, where labor supply, and therefore incomes, are variable. When labor supply is fixed these more general tax systems can circumvent entirely the problem of endogenous fertility, which is why we restrict the analysis in this section to the simple family-based tax system.
3. For the sake of simplicity, we do not consider nonlinear taxes. When fertility is not endogenous, the analysis reduces to the standard one; see Mirrlees (1976).

## References

Balcer, Yves and Efraim Sadka (1982), "Horizontal Equity, Income Taxation and Self-Selection with an Application to Income Tax Credits." *Journal of Public Economics*, **19**, 291–309.

Becker, G. S. and H. G. Lewis (1973), "On the Interaction between the Quantity and Quality of Children." *Journal of Political Economy*, **81**, 279–88.

Bruno, M. and J. Habib (1976), "Taxes, Family Grants and Redistribution." *Journal of Public Economics*, **5**, 57–80.

Deaton, A. and J. Muellbauer (1983), "On Measuring Child Costs in Poor Countries." Mimeo.

Mirrlees, J. A. (1971), "An exploration in the Theory of Optimum Income Taxation." *Review of Economic Studies*, **38**, 175–208.

Mirrlees, J. A. (1972), "Population Policy and the Taxation of Family Size." *Journal of Public Economics*, **1**, 169–98.

Mirrlees, J. A. (1976), "Optimal Tax Theory: A Synthesis." *Journal of Public Economics*, **6**, 327–58.

Musgrave, R. A. (1959), *The Theory of Public Finance*. New York: McGraw-Hill.

Pechman, J. A. (1966), *Federal Tax Policy*. New York: W. W. Norton and Co.

Sadka, Efraim (1976), "On Income Distribution, Incentive Effects and Optimal Income Taxation." *Review of Economic Studies*, **43**, 261–67.

Schultz, T. W. (ed.) (1974), *Economics of the Family: Marriage, Children and Human Capital*. Chicago and London: National Bureau of Economic Research.

# Epilogue

This book has explored the implications of endogenous determination of fertility for certain issues in population policy. By endogenous fertility we mean something rather different from endogenous population size. The consequences of endogenous fertility for many issues of population policy are far-reaching. With respect to the socially optimal size of a population, we asked whether a maximization of the sum of parents' and children's utilities leads to a higher rate of population growth than maximization of the per-capita total. We also asked whether the laissez-faire solution (equivalent to maximizing a social welfare function that gives weight only to the utilities of the present generation) leads necessarily to a higher rate of growth than the maximization of per-capita utility or to a lower rate than the maximization of total utility. The reason for a possible ambiguity is a direct consequence of the endogeneity of fertility for the current generation. Indeed, there is no laissez-faire solution unless children are directly or indirectly valued by parents. We considered alternative noncoercive policies to support various allocations, such as child allowances, interest rate subsidies, etc.

We also considered the implications of endogenous fertility for market failure, i.e., the failure of the laissez-faire allocation to achieve Pareto efficiency for the current generation. We noted that two potential sources of externalities, diminishing returns and public goods, do not lead to market failure; since parents care about their children, the sources of externalities are internalized in parental fertility decisions. However, parental concern for the welfare of their children may give rise to other sorts of externalities, among which are those associated with marriage of children and variations in the ability of offspring. We explored noncoercive social policies to correct or offset the effects of such externalities.

When children are not valued for their own sake but only as a device for transferring resources from present to future consumption, some researchers hypothesize that introduction of an alternative form of saving will reduce population growth. We showed that this theory is false when general equilibrium effects are taken into account. Furthermore, even if one ignores such effects when fertility is endogenous because parents care about their children, relaxation of the constraint to saving in forms other than children creates a positive income effect, and parents may still bring more children into the world.

Endogenous fertility also has implications for intragenerational income distribution policies, since such policies affect both the number and quality of individuals in successive generations. For example, even if poor people tend to substitute numbers of children for investments in child quality, positive child allowances may still be optimal for redistributing income within the current generation. The optimality of child allowances as a means of income redistribution may be affected, however, by the interaction of endogenous fertility with labor supply decisions. These issues are very important for the incorporation of demographic elements in an optimal tax system.

In this book we have explored only the simplest feature of endogenous fertility. As a postscript to this investigation, we outline several promising directions of further investigation: (1) general theory of tax and transfer policies that consider family size and composition; (2) alternative provision and finance of public goods; (3) intragenerational income distribution with household production and endogenous fertility; (4) heterogenous family preferences; and (5) uncertainty with respect to child quality.

## 1.  Tax and Transfer Policies

An extension of our basic model to emphasize the population aspects (quantity and quality) of tax policies can be made as follows. One wants to devise an income tax schedule that depends on family income, family size and age composition, and quality improving expenditure. Consider a stylized overlapping generations model in which each family lives for three periods: a representative individual is born in period 1, during which he or she has no income of his or her own; the individual works (earning $I$, which depends on the individual's human capital stock) and bears children in period 2; the individual retires in period 3. In period 1, all decisions with regard to consumption, education, and so forth are made by the individual's parents. In period 2, the individual decides the number of children to have $(n)$ and how much to invest in them $(z)$, how much the family shall consume $(c_2)$, and how much to save for retirement $(s)$. In period 3, the individual decides how much accumulated savings plus any transfer income (social security benefits) to consume $(c_3)$ and how much to bequeath to his or her children $(b)$.

A general tax-transfer function can be represented by a vector function,

$$T = (T_2, T_3) = (T_2(I, n, z, s), T_3(s(1 + r), b)).$$

where $r$ is the interest rate. This function incorporates various tax-transfer instruments, such as income or consumption taxes, social security taxes, inheritance taxes, social security benefits, child allowances or deductions, educational subsidies or deductions, etc. For example, an income tax prevails when $T_2$ depends on $I$ and does not depend on $s$; a consumption tax is obtained when $T_2$ depends on $I - s$. Child deductions are incorporated by making $T_2$ depend on $I - n\beta$, where $\beta$ is the per capita child exemption. In the third period, $T_3$ represents the *net* tax payments, which may be negative if social security payments outweigh tax payments. An inheritance tax is represented by having $T_3$ depend on $b$.

Extending our model—by evaluating a number of possible specific forms of this general tax function, assessing the implications of each tax policy on family behavior, and deriving the optimal tax policy—at last put the treatment of family size and composition in the *theory* of taxation on a firm microeconomic basis.

## 2. Public Goods and Dynasty Taxes

In Chapter 7 we assumed that the government provides the public goods in each period and finances them by a lump-sum tax $(T)$ that is imposed on the dynasty as a whole. (This approach is necessary because a head tax is not a lump-sum tax in our model since the number of children is endogenous.) Under this assumption, we showed that the existence of public goods does not lead to market failure. On the other hand, a head tax on individual members of each generation is obviously distortionary when fertility is endogenous and will, in general, lead to market failure. If a tax on each dynasty is ruled out, one may consider two alternatives.

First, the public good may be financed by a tax on land rent (pure economic profit). In this case, there will be no market failure provided that there is enough rent on land to finance the public good. Indeed, the theory of local public finance (the "Henry George Rule") suggests that if the quantity of each public good is set optimally at each point in time, then a 100 percent tax on land rent will be just sufficient to finance provision of the good. This theory, however, has not been developed in the case of endogenous fertility and the "Rule" is not obviously true. Can a first-best solution to the problem of providing public goods be achieved if a tax on each dynasty is ruled out?

Second, with no dynasty taxes and no full optimal provision of public goods through land taxes, one can consider second-best solutions, among them those achieved through head taxes on individual members of each generation, income taxes, interest taxes, taxes on labor income, inheritance taxes, child allowances and taxes, etc. In doing so, one could develop a theory of the second-best optimal provision of public goods, population size, and tax financing.

As discussed in Chapter 7, if marriages are allowed *between* dynasties, then a market failure can arise. In this case, children who marry children from another dynasty reduce the average tax burden on each original member of the other dynasty, and vice versa. Thus, there is an external economy to the number of children that is not internalized by the heads of dynasties. A similar kind of externality associated with marriage also applies to intergenerational transfers: the transfer that parents make to their child also benefits the parents of the spouse of the child. We considered this particular issue in Chapter 8, but the same framework can be easily applied to study the external economy due to interdynasty marriage that arises in the presence of public goods.

### 3. Intragenerational Income Distribution with Household Production and Endogenous Fertility

In Chapter 10 we deal with some implications of endogenous fertility for intragenerational welfare comparisons of alternative policies with respect to income taxation and family allowances. In further research it would be important to take account of the determinants of fertility beyond merely including the number and quality of children in a reduced form of the utility function and the budget constraints of the family. In particular, it may prove useful to use a household production function to determine the allocation of time and resources within a family among market activities, child rearing, and other activities. Such analysis has important implications for the determination of tax policies concerning the treatment of the number of children, for first and second wage earners in families, for the age of wage earners and children, etc. This kind of analysis may be extended in the context of the Becker-Lancaster theory of time allocation and household production.

## 4.   Heterogeneous Family Preferences

In all of the work to date on population size and bequest, the assumption that a single utility function represents family preferences has generally been maintained. But it may be far more appropriate to consider different objectives for husbands and wives, which may generate intrafamily conflicts and necessitate a contractural or other theory of household behavior.

## 5.   Uncertainty with Respect to Child Quality

In Chapter 8 we dealt with some issues raised by heterogeneous child quality. Given constraints on the ability of parents to enforce transfers among their offspring, laissez-faire leads to a genuine market failure; among several policy alternatives, we found that a tax on earned income can lead to an improved distribution of welfare among members of the current generation.

If child quality, in the sense of being able to absorb investment in human capital productivity, is uncertain *ex ante*, new difficulties arise. If the uncertainty pertains only to individual families but not collectively, it is possible to design a social insurance scheme that will permit an optimal solution with respect to numbers of children, investment in them, and bequests of nonhuman capital. How should such a first-best insurance policy be characterized? If for reasons of moral hazard or other problems, insurance is ruled out, what are the second-best alternatives, such as taxes on earned income, etc.?

Such extensions and deepening of our analysis lie in the future. The present work, we believe, makes a contribution in showing that a fuller integration of the empirical and theoretical insights of the "new home economics" into a general equilibrium and welfare theoretic analysis of population growth and the relations among generations has a high payoff.

# Author Index

# Subject Index

# ECONOMIC THEORY, ECONOMETRICS, AND MATHEMATICAL ECONOMICS

Consulting Editor: Karl Shell